AF255011

BUYER SENSE CONVERSATIONS

How Founders Help Buyers Make
Confident Decisions in Complex B2B Deals

Petra Wagner

To Matija, Lana, Izabela, and Valentin—
thank you for your endless love, patience, and time.

PRAISE FOR BUYER SENSE CONVERSATIONS

"This wellcrafted framework equips visionary founders with the structure and insight needed to drive lasting success and powerful sales momentum."

Ludo Wijckmans
Scale-Up Expert & Board Advisor
Founder, StartExpand

"A brilliant guide to decoding the buyer's mind. Petra combines psychological insight with actionable strategy, creating a blueprint for anyone who wants to stop selling and start partnering."

Robert Trnovec
Senior Executive, Technology & Financial Services

During my 20-year corporate career, I've been on both sides of the table — as a buyer and as a seller — and I've experienced the struggles from each perspective.

What this book does brilliantly is make sense of not only the internal buying process inside organizations, but also the human side of the selling–buying dynamic — the part that is so often overlooked. I work with startups every day and see firsthand how challenging B2B sales can be for early-stage founders. I've also sat through countless sales workshops and listened to many gurus promote approaches that simply don't work for startups — or don't work at all.

What I like about the book most is a clear, actionable "how-to" guidance part. It's not theory — it's usable. This book is definitely going on my must-read list for every founder serious about selling to B2B customers.

Maja Križan
COO at Business angels of Slovenia
Operations Manager at Vesna Deep tech Venture Fund
Coach

FOREWORD
BY GRAHAM HAWKINS

I've known Petra Wagner long enough to tell you this with absolute confidence: she doesn't have opinions about B2B sales—she has earned conclusions.

We've worked together, invested together, and spent time in rooms with founders and sales teams who are genuinely trying to figure out how to sell in a world that feels more complex, risk averse, and buyer driven than ever before. And in every one of those environments, Petra brings the same rare combination of clarity, empathy, and absolute credibility.

Yes, she's an internationally respected sales leader. Yes, she's worked for global technology companies like Microsoft and IBM. And, yes, she's operated across markets, cultures, and buying environments with impressive consistency. But those things alone don't explain why her thinking resonates so deeply with modern sellers all around the world.

The real reason is simple: Petra understands B2B buyers because *she has been one*.

Petra knows that buying decisions are rarely clean or linear. They're shaped by uncertainty, business and personal risk, internal politics, and the very human fear of making the wrong call—especially when decisions are shared across groups. She understands that buyers don't stall because they're disengaged, and they don't default to "no" because they dislike sellers. More often, they pause because they're still trying to understand what, exactly, they're deciding, what problem they are solving, and whether they can defend that decision later.

That insight runs through this entire book.

At a time when sellers are under pressure to move faster, deliver more, and prove value earlier than ever, Petra makes a compelling case for something that feels almost counterintuitive: that progress comes from slowing down and helping buyers make sense of complexity.

Not about solutions, but about problems. Not about features, but about trade-offs. Not about individual conversations, but about the shared understanding buying groups need in order to move forward together.

This is the heart of *Buyer Sense Conversations*. When buyers feel clear and safe, decisions move forward—not because buyers are convinced, but because they're confident. It's not about persuading buyers to choose you. It's about helping them navigate the buying process to arrive at a decision they can feel confident about. It's solving, not selling.

Today's buyers are navigating more risk, more information, more internal scrutiny, and more choice than at any point in recent memory. In that environment, pushing harder doesn't create momentum—it creates resistance. Petra's work speaks directly to this reality, offering founders and sellers a practical, structured way to guide B2B buyers toward clarity, alignment, and confidence—without the pressure, persuasion tactics, or manipulation.

I've seen this approach land in real situations. I've watched founders have breakthrough moments when they realize they weren't losing deals because their solution wasn't strong enough, but because they were unintentionally overwhelming the very people they were trying to help: those all-important early adopters (their buyers). Petra has an extraordinary ability to surface these moments—not by undermining the role of the seller, but by reframing how they see the buying experience itself.

I've also had the privilege of working alongside Petra in Slovenia and the UK, delivering Modern Selling workshops together. In every context, Petra brings the same integrity to her work: thoughtful, practical, and grounded in a deep understanding of the buyer's reality.

This book doesn't offer tactics designed to "close" buyers. It offers something far more valuable for the times we're in: a way to help B2B buyers feel clear, aligned, and confident enough to move forward—even in complex, high-stakes decisions.

In a world where buyers are overwhelmed with information, Petra teaches sellers how to create clarity. And clarity is what drives buying decisions.

If you care about selling in a way that reflects how decisions are actually made today—and how they will be made tomorrow—then you're in very good hands.

I'm proud to call Petra a collaborator, an investor, and a friend.

—Graham Hawkins

TABLE OF CONTENTS

PART I
PSYCHOLOGY & FOUNDATIONS

PART III
APPLICATION & TOOLS

THE MOMENT EVERYTHING BROKE

The meeting room was quiet in the way only corporate spaces can be: still, expectant, a little too polished. A long wooden table stretched across the center, its eight perfectly aligned chairs creating a sense of order I rarely felt anywhere else in the organization. This was the room where strategies were debated, budgets were rewired, and decisions quietly shaped the next chapter of the company. It had a presence, a weight. And on that afternoon, I found myself feeling that weight more than usual.

I wasn't sitting behind my desk or leading a team, as I had for so many years. I wasn't coaching a seller or preparing for a pitch. I wasn't thinking in slides or deal forecasts or pipeline pressure. I was sitting on the opposite side of the table, in the seat I had taught others to navigate for decades. I was the buyer.

What struck me immediately, and somewhat surprisingly, was how unfamiliar that seat felt. After two decades at IBM and Microsoft—living inside enterprise sales, partner ecosystems, transformation initiatives, and complex account planning—I assumed I understood the buyer's world. I believed I knew their pressures, their priorities, their limitations. But the moment I crossed into this role, the ground shifted under my feet. Suddenly, I was the one carrying the responsibility of decisions that would disrupt long-standing habits, challenge deeply rooted ways of working, and require people who had not moved in years to move now.

We were in the middle of a major transformation. Not the shiny kind celebrated on conference stages, but the real kind that happens inside traditional organizations where the average IT employee is nearly fifty and has been in the same role for over fifteen years. Change did not flow easily through this place; it moved like thick liquid through narrow pipes. Everything required negotiation. Every improvement threatened someone's comfort. And while the company needed a new direction, the burden of getting it right and not breaking something essential sat heavily on my shoulders.

Across from me sat a startup founder, young and eager, eyes full of possibility. His laptop was open before he had even finished introducing himself. I recognized that energy instantly: the mixture of hope, drive, and nerves that only early-stage founders carry. A part of me respected it deeply, as I know what it means to build something from nothing. And another part of me, the part responsible for transformation inside a traditional enterprise, felt a quiet and very real fear.

Because the truth buyers rarely admit—even to themselves—is that choosing a startup is not only a technical or financial decision. It is a personal risk. I was silently asking myself questions the founder could not see:

- *"What if their product can't handle our complexity?"*
- *"What if they don't survive the year?"*
- *"What if this choice derails the transformation I am responsible for?"*
- *"What if I choose wrong, and I alone carry the consequences?"*

He began his pitch with confidence. "Let me show you our roadmap," he said. And then came the slides. They were dense, intricate, and impressive in their own way, but they were far removed from the world I was navigating. Features, modules, architecture diagrams, and integration pathways were all delivered with the steady rhythm of someone who had been told this was how you demonstrate value.

I waited for the moment when he would pause and invite me in—ask a question, acknowledge my environment, or explore what we were trying to accomplish. I waited for a sign that we were in a conversation, not a presentation. But the moment never came.

The more he spoke, the more I felt a quiet distance open between us. On his laptop was the future as he imagined it. In my mind was the reality I had to defend.

After several minutes, I leaned forward gently. "Can you help me understand the business impact?" He nodded, energetically, almost gratefully—and clicked to the next feature slide. He didn't answer my question. He didn't even seem to notice that he hadn't answered it.

And in that moment, something shifted inside me. It wasn't irritation, although there was some of that. It wasn't disappointment, though I felt that too. It was the sudden clarity that this seller, who genuinely cared, who believed in his product, who was doing everything he had been taught to do, simply could not see the world I was sitting in. It wasn't that he was ignoring my context. It was that he didn't know how to recognize it.

And the deeper truth landed quietly: **The only reason I could interpret his pitch was that I had lived in his world. A typical buyer would drown.** I asked another question, a more practical one. "How would this actually work in our environment?"

He hesitated, then offered another vague explanation wrapped in buzzwords. And in that pause, I understood the real gap. It wasn't in his solution, but in the conversation.

He thought he was explaining value, while I was trying to understand risk. He thought he was showing innovation, while I was trying to assess defensibility. He thought he was selling software, while I was deciding whether I could stand behind this decision in a room far more demanding than this one.

By the time the meeting ended, I knew I couldn't move forward. He left relieved, believing he had delivered everything he needed to. And I sat alone at the long table, surrounded by the quiet realization that something fundamental in modern selling was broken.

I called someone else from his company, a person who had known me from my years in enterprise sales. In twenty minutes, he translated the entire pitch into the language of my reality: risks, dependencies, constraints, political terrain, impact. Twenty minutes gave me the clarity the formal meeting had never reached.

That's when the final insight surfaced, clean and sharp: **Buyers are not overwhelmed because they lack information. They're overwhelmed because sellers don't help them make sense of the information.** That moment became the beginning of this book. Not as a sales methodology. Not as a set of techniques. Not as another model in a crowded field. It became a promise I made to myself: *If sellers could learn to guide buyers through clarity rather than noise, everything about modern sales would change.*

This book is the fulfillment of that promise. It is a guide for founders and sellers who want to lead conversations that restore clarity, reduce uncertainty, and help buyers move with confidence in a world that often feels unstable and overloaded. Because clarity is not a tactic. Clarity is leadership. And buyers follow the person who brings it into the room.

WHY I WROTE THIS BOOK

Most startup founders don't struggle with sales because they lack intelligence, ambition, or courage. In fact, founders are often some of the most capable people in the room—sharp thinkers with deep domain knowledge and an intimate understanding of the problem they set out to solve. Their challenge is not ability, but rather the *game* they've been taught to play.

Traditional sales was never designed for founders. It was built for professional salespeople operating inside large organizations, supported by brand recognition, marketing engines, established trust, and decades of reputation. These sellers stand on the shoulders of systems that speak for them long before they enter the room. Founders do not have that luxury.

When you are the founder, you are selling with no warm trust behind you. You have no well-known logo to lean on, no established credibility that buys you a few extra seconds of grace, often no clear solution category to anchor to, and very often, no formal sales training at all. Yet despite this, you are expected to persuade skeptical buyers, navigate internal politics, interpret unclear signals, and guide complex decisions inside organizations that struggle to move even when the need is obvious.

That's why I wrote this book.

Founders need a different approach, one that matches their natural strengths rather than forcing them into someone else's playbook. The skills that make you a powerful founder are the same skills that make you a powerful seller: your ability to see patterns other people miss, your strategic curiosity, your authenticity, your lived experience with the problem, and your point of view about what needs to change.

You don't need to become a traditional salesperson. You need to become a *sensemaker*, someone who helps buyers think more clearly than they can on their own.

As the opening story illustrated, modern buyers are not looking for more information. They do not really care what your product can do. What they want is someone who can help them understand what truly matters to their business and what a good decision looks like in their reality.

That is the role you are meant to play.

- You do not need scripts.
- You do not need pressure tactics.
- You do not need to pretend to be someone you're not.

You need a way of helping people think.

If you can do that, not only will you sell more effectively, but you will become the kind of leader buyers trust, follow, and invite into their most important decisions.

WHAT THIS BOOK WILL TEACH YOU

This book will teach you *how* to lead conversations that bring clarity into complex situations. It will show you how to help buyers uncover the problems they are having, so you can show them the exact ways your solution can help them. Even more, you will learn to help them convey that value across different stakeholders.

In these pages you will learn how to:

- **Understand How Buyers Actually Decide Today**
  See how decisions move inside real organizations, and what has to become true internally before a team commits.

- **See the Problem Beneath the Problem**
  Hear beyond surface requests and spot the deeper patterns shaping what the buyer is experiencing.

- **Guide Buyers Through the Buyer Sense Flow**
  Use the seven decision transitions—ORIENT → DECODE → DISTURB → REFRAME → ALIGN → PRIORITIZE → MOBILIZE—to help buyers move from uncertainty to confident action.

- **Ask Questions That Create Insight**
  Use sensemaking questions that help buyers reflect, articulate, interpret, and connect the dots—without turning the call into an interrogation.

- **Create Clarity Across Stakeholders**
  Navigate misalignment, competing interpretations, workflow friction, and politics to move a group toward shared understanding.

- **Build Momentum When You're Not There**
  Equip internal champions and shape the internal narrative so progress continues in the meetings you don't attend.
- **Sell Without Feeling Like You're Selling**
  Lead conversations that feel collaborative and grounded, helping buyers choose—and defend—their decision with confidence.

By the end of this book, you will know how to guide complex B2B conversations with structure, confidence, and emotional intelligence, even if you have never seen yourself as a salesperson.

How to Read This Book (and How to Use It)

Buyer Sense Conversations™ is not designed to be consumed quickly.

If you are looking for shortcuts, scripts, or immediately deployable tactics, this book may feel demanding at first. That reaction is intentional. This book does not simplify complexity away. It teaches you how to work inside it with clarity.

Buyer Sense Conversations is organized into three distinct parts:

Part I helps you see modern buying accurately and interpret stalled deals without guessing or adding pressure.

Part II introduces the Buyer Sense Conversations framework. The seven stages reflect the internal work buyers must complete to move from uncertainty to confident action. Use them to identify what is missing when you lose momentum and what kind of clarity the buyer needs next.

Part III focuses on application. This is where the framework becomes practical: how to prepare for conversations, how to recognize failure modes, how to support internal alignment, and how to help decisions survive inside the buyer's organization after the call ends.

This is not a book you are meant to sound like.

Buyer Sense Conversations is not about adopting language, phrases, or a performance style. If you try to "sound like the book," buyers will feel it immediately, and you will lose the very thing that makes founders powerful sellers: your natural authority on your solution and your lived relationship with the problem.

Buyer Sense Conversations is not traditional sales.

It may feel less forceful than approaches like Challenger because it doesn't lead with disruption, early insight, or urgency. That's deliberate. In complex buying, challenge only lands after trust and safety are in place. Buyer Sense earns that first by proving you understand the buyer's reality, then co-creates the reframe. For early-stage founders, that difference matters: early customers aren't just buyers—they're learning partners.

One final orientation before you begin.

Buyer Sense Conversations will sharpen how you think, but you will only see results when you practice what is taught. Sensemaking is a skill built through repetition, reflection, and real application— especially when stakes are high and clarity is fragile.

Don't rush this book. Revisit sections after real conversations. Notice what shifts when you slow down, ask differently, and help buyers make sense of their world instead of trying to convince them of your solution. If parts feel challenging, that's not failure— it means you are dealing with the same complexity your buyers face every day.

That is exactly where *Buyer Sense Conversations* begins.

A NOTE ON PRACTICE SUPPORT: PETRA AI

Buyer Sense Conversations™ is a way of thinking before it is a way of speaking.

Most founders understand this framework conceptually long before they can apply it consistently in real buyer conversations. In practice, conversations are rarely clean or linear. They are shaped by uncertainty, internal alignment issues, competing priorities, political exposure, and emotional risk. When buyers hesitate or slow down, even experienced founders tend to fall back on familiar patterns—explaining more, pushing for momentum, or trying to "fix" uncertainty instead of understanding it.

Sensemaking is not developed through reading alone. It forms through reflection, repetition, and guided application. Petra AI exists to support that learning process.

Petra AI is a practice partner designed to help you work with this book before, between, and after real buyer conversations. It helps you turn insight into usable judgment by slowing your thinking without slowing progress, so clarity can emerge where pressure often takes over.

Petra AI supports founders on two connected levels.

At the **system level**, Petra AI is trained on the SalesBooster™ Framework. This level focuses on structure: how you define your ideal customers, how value is framed, how opportunities progress, and where deals tend to stall or drift. Petra AI helps you examine the internal logic of your sales system so decisions about focus, prioritization, and next steps are grounded in clarity rather than habit or hope.

At the **conversation level**, Petra AI is trained on the Buyer Sense Conversations™ framework. Here, the focus shifts from selling activity to buyer sensemaking. Petra AI helps you interpret what is happening inside the buyer's decision process—where clarity is forming, where risk is accumulating, and how your behavior influences whether decisions feel safe enough to move forward.

Founders use Petra AI to reflect on real buyer interactions, especially those that feel confusing, tense, or stalled. They use it to map conversations to the Buyer Sense stages, translate fragmented buyer input into a coherent internal narrative, and test whether advancing the conversation would support clarity, or introduce pressure too early.

How Founders Work With Petra AI

Founders use Petra AI to:

- Reflect on real buyer conversations that feel unclear or stuck
- Sense-check where a buyer actually is in the Buyer Sense journey
- Translate partial, ambiguous buyer input into a clear internal narrative
- Pressure test whether it is time to advance—or time to stay exactly where they are
- Practice how to guide clarity without adding urgency or pressure

If you are new to working with AI, think of Petra AI as someone you can talk *with*, not something you need to "prompt correctly." You do not need special commands or technical language. Start with the situation in front of you.

For example, you might explore:

- "Here's what the buyer said in our last call. What might be happening for them internally?"
- "Based on this conversation, where does the buyer seem to be in the Buyer Sense journey?"
- "What signals suggest growing clarity, and what signals suggest unresolved risk?"
- "Am I trying to move this decision forward too early? What tells me that?"
- "Where might my behavior be increasing decision risk without me realizing it?"
- "How could I respond next time in a way that supports clarity rather than urgency?"

These are not scripts to follow. They are starting points for sensemaking—helping you see buyer situations more accurately, so your next move is guided by understanding rather than pressure.

Petra AI does not replace judgment. It strengthens it. Over time, it helps insight become repeatable and instinctive, so you can navigate complex buyer situations with greater confidence and consistency.

If you choose to use Petra AI, think of it as a sensemaking companion rather than a performance tool. It is something you work with privately, between conversations, as you develop the ability to guide decisions without forcing them.

You can explore Petra AI at: https://petrasalesbooster.com/new-petra-ai.

Its purpose is simple: to help insight turn into instinct.

PSYCHOLOGY & FOUNDATIONS

Part I resets how you see modern B2B buying—by explaining the buyer and founder psychology behind decision paralysis—and introduces sensemaking as the foundation you'll use in Part II to guide real Buyer Sense Conversations.

THE PROBLEM – MODERN BUYING REALITY AND BUYER DECISION PARALYSIS

1.1 The Deal That Didn't Lose to a Competitor

The call went well.

The buyer showed up with real energy. They asked thoughtful questions. They nodded at the right moments. They even said the sentence founders secretly wait for: "This feels like exactly what we need."

You left the meeting thinking, *This is moving.*

Then the week passed.

No follow-up. No calendar hold. No objections. No competitor mentioned. Just a polite silence that felt heavier than a "no."

If you've lived through this pattern, you already know the most confusing part: it rarely feels like you lost. It feels like the decision evaporated somewhere inside the customer's organization—after the meeting, in the internal rooms you never enter.

That outcome is no longer the exception. Forrester reports that **86% of B2B purchases stall during the buying process**, and a large majority of buyers finish the process dissatisfied with the provider they chose.[1]

Chapter 1 is here to name the environment that creates those stalls—clearly, directly, and with proof. Because once you see the real problem, the rest of the book makes sense.

1.2 The Five Forces Behind Decision Paralysis

Modern deals do not stall because buyers lack options. They stall because buyers struggle to build a decision that holds up internally—across stakeholders, constraints, and risk.

Five forces explain most of the paralysis founders experience.

A) You Get a Thin Slice of the Buying Time

Gartner reports that buyers spend **only 17% of their time meeting with potential suppliers** during a purchase.[2]

That number carries a blunt implication: most of the decision is built without you. Most of the work happens in internal discussions, in async threads, in partial meetings, and in quick hallway alignment moments that never include a founder.

This creates a mismatch between what founders think is happening and what's actually happening. Founders assume the decision will move forward because the conversation was strong. Buyers assume the decision will move forward only if they can translate that conversation into internal agreement.

---

1. Forrester, *The State of Business Buying*, 2024 – 86% of B2B purchases stall during the buying process, and 81% of buyers express dissatisfaction with the provider they chose.

2. Gartner, "Gartner Says 80% of B2B Sales Interactions Between Suppliers and Buyers Will Occur in Digital Channels by 2025," 2020 – buyers typically spend only 17% of their time meeting with potential suppliers when considering a purchase.

So when a buyer says, "This is great," what they often mean is, "This is plausible." The real question becomes: *Can we carry this forward inside our organization without getting exposed?*

B) High-Quality Information Increases Uncertainty

Gartner found that **89% of customers encounter high-quality information** during the purchase process.[3] And yet, when customers struggle to make sense of that information, they become more likely to choose a path that is **smaller or less disruptive** than what they originally intended.[4]

This is one of the most important shifts in modern selling: more information does not reliably create more clarity.

Founders feel this every time a buyer asks for "one more deck," "one more case study," or "one more comparison," and the deal gets slower instead of faster. The buyer is not collecting facts. They are trying to resolve internal uncertainty. If the information stays unorganized, conflicting, or politically hard to interpret, it adds friction instead of reducing it.

In other words: your buyer can be well-informed and still feel unsafe moving forward.

C) Buying Is a Group Alignment Problem

Forrester reports that, on average, **13 people** are involved in a buying decision, and **89% of purchases involve two or more departments**.[5]

---

3. **Gartner, "Customer Confidence," 2019** – 89% of customers encounter high-quality information during the purchase process; when customers struggle to make sense of it, they are more likely to purchase a smaller, less disruptive option than originally intended.

4. Ibid – when customers struggle to make sense of that information, they become more likely to choose a path that is smaller or less disruptive than what they originally intended.

5. **Forrester, "Buying Committees Have 13 Stakeholders," 2024** – an average

This is why having a "strong internal champion" is no longer enough. The buyer's world is cross-functional by default. Every additional stakeholder brings a different view of risk, a different definition of success, and a different incentive.

Even when everyone agrees a problem exists, they often disagree on what the problem *is*.

- Finance hears cost, spend, and trade-offs.
- Security hears exposure and control.
- Operations hears disruption and workload.
- Leadership hears strategy, timing, and reputational risk.
- Users hear friction, change, and learning curves.

Founders often experience this as "late-stage complexity." Buyers experience it as "the real work."

A deal does not move when one person is convinced. It moves when a group can share a coherent interpretation and a defensible story.

D) "No Decision" Is a Primary Outcome

Harvard Business Review reports that **40% to 60% of deals** are lost to customers who express intent to buy but ultimately **fail to act**.[6]

This is the moment founders misread most often. "No decision" rarely feels like rejection. It feels like delay. It feels like the buyer is busy. It feels like procurement is slow. It feels like timing.

In reality, "no decision" usually signals an internal breakdown: the buyer could not complete the internal work required to commit.

---

of 13 people are involved in a buying decision; 89% of purchases involve two or more departments.

6. **Dixon & McKenna, "Stop Losing Sales to Customer Indecision," Harvard Business Review, 2022** – 40% to 60% of deals are lost to customers who express intent to buy but ultimately fail to act ("no decision").

According to **Kahneman & Tversky this is often caused by the fact that** loss aversion leads people to overweight downside risk 2-3 times more than equivalent upside.[7]

They could not build alignment. They could not defend trade-offs. They could not make the decision safe enough to carry.

And because that internal work is invisible to vendors, founders often try to fix the stall with outward effort: more follow-ups, more proof, more urgency, more pressure. That tends to create additional friction, because it adds energy to the conversation without reducing the uncertainty underneath it.

E) Regret Is High, So Buyers Optimize for Defensibility

Gartner found that **60% of technology buyers** involved in renewal or expansion decisions regret nearly every purchase they make.[8] Gartner also reports that these feelings are driven largely by distributed buying teams and the challenges of buying with misaligned stakeholders and funding.[9]

This is what modern fear looks like in B2B: not fear of missing out, but fear of being stuck with the consequences.

When regret is common, buyers become conservative in predictable ways:

- They avoid decisions that create visible personal exposure.
- They lean toward incremental choices they can justify.
- They seek options that feel reversible.

---

7. Kahneman & Tversky, Econometrica, 1979 – loss aversion leads people to overweight downside risk (often ~2× versus equivalent upside).

8. **Gartner, "60% of Buyers Regret Nearly Every Purchase," 2023** – 60% of technology buyers involved in renewal/expansion decisions regret nearly every purchase; regret is driven largely by distributed buying teams and funding.

9. Ibid. – Gartner also reports that these feelings are driven largely by distributed buying teams and the challenges of buying with misaligned stakeholders and funding.

- They delay until the story is solid enough to withstand scrutiny.

This also explains why buyers can sound excited in a meeting and still hesitate afterward. Enthusiasm is not the same as internal safety. Many buyers can genuinely like your solution while still feeling unable to defend the move inside their organization.

1.3 The Confidence Crisis: Three Interlocking Layers

When founders describe modern selling, they often describe skepticism: "Buyers don't trust vendors."

That is part of the picture, but it is not the core problem.

Gartner's research points to something more fundamental: the biggest challenge is a lack of customer confidence—specifically, the buyer's confidence in **their own ability to make a good decision**, especially in an environment of abundant and conflicting information.[10]

This reframes the founder's role.

In a decision-confidence environment, the buyer is not mainly asking, "Is this vendor credible?" They are also asking, "Can we make this choice and feel good about it later?"

They want a decision that holds up in three places:

1. In their own mind
2. Across their stakeholders
3. In front of leadership scrutiny

---

10. **Gartner, "60% of Buyers Regret Nearly Every Purchase," 2023 –** the biggest challenge is a lack of customer confidence—specifically, the buyer's confidence in their own ability to make a good decision, especially in an environment of abundant and conflicting information.

But three interlocking layers keep confidence from forming:

1. Overwhelm – too many options, conflicting inputs, unclear information.

The average B2B buying committee reviews information from nearly a dozen sources. They struggle to reconcile conflicting data points, internal opinions, and shifting priorities. Decision fatigue sets in long before evaluation even begins.

2. Internal Misalignment – multiple stakeholders, competing priorities.

McKinsey's research shows that the number of stakeholders involved in a typical B2B decision has doubled in the last decade. When teams cannot agree on the definition of the problem, they cannot agree on the solution either. Misalignment makes inaction feel like the safest option.

3. Personal Risk – fear of being blamed if the initiative fails.

Harvard Business Review notes that buyers overweight downside risk by 2–3×. This fear is not purely rational—it is political and emotional. Buyers worry more about regret, exposure, and credibility than they worry about missing out on an opportunity.

This is the real enemy in modern sales—not competitors. Your competition is buyer uncertainty.

If any one of those collapses, the deal stalls—often without visible warning.

This is the hidden engine behind modern buying paralysis: buyers are trying to turn complexity into coherence. When they cannot, they choose delay.

1.4 The Modern Buying Environment Map

Figure 1: The Modern Buying Environment Map

Figure 1 illustrates why buying stalls even when the solution is strong. At the center is the buyer—not as a rational evaluator of vendors, but as a human decision-maker absorbing pressure from multiple directions.

- **External complexity** includes shifting priorities, tight budgets, market uncertainty, regulatory pressure, and constant organizational change.
- **Internal misalignment** includes competing agendas

across departments, unclear ownership, and different interpretations of the same problem.

- **Information overload** includes abundant high-quality content that still fails to resolve trade-offs or provide a clear path forward.
- **Personal risk** sits closest to the buyer because every decision carries exposure: credibility, career risk, and the burden of being associated with the outcome.

Together, these forces compound. The result is decision overload. When buyers cannot reduce this complexity into a story they can defend internally, progress slows, stalls, or disappears.

1.5 The Internal Buyer Journey: What Happens After Your Meeting

A sales conversation is visible. The buyer's decision work is mostly invisible.

Gartner's 17% finding we mentioned earlier makes this unavoidable: after your meeting ends, the buyer's work intensifies.[11] The buyer must translate a conversation into something an organization can commit to.

That internal journey tends to move through three transitions. They are not steps in your sales process. They are the buyer's internal work.

---

11. **Gartner, "80% of B2B Sales Interactions Will Be Digital by 2025," 2020 –** buyers spend only 17% of their buying time meeting with potential suppliers.

INTERNAL BUYER JOURNEY

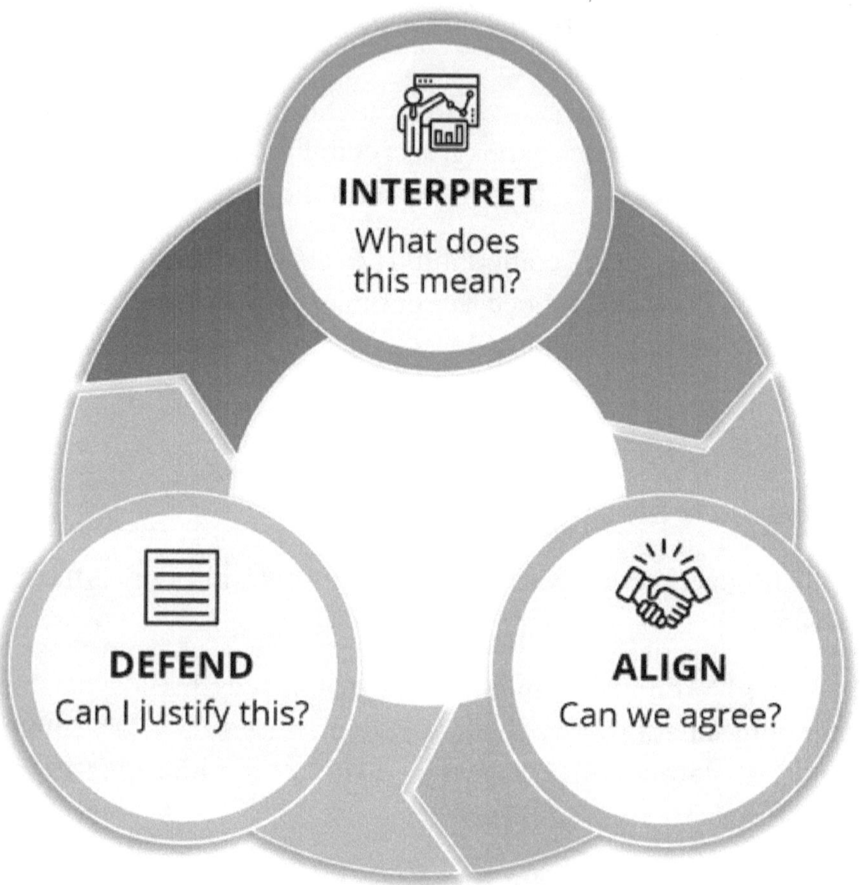

Figure 2: Internal Buyer Journey

1) Interpret: "What does this mean for us?"

Before a buyer can sell anything internally, they must make sense of it privately.

They are trying to answer questions like:

- What problem did we just name, in plain language?

- How big it it? How costly?
- Where does it show up in our system?
- Does this match what I see day-to-day?
- It this even the right problem to be talking about?

This is where many deals quietly stall. Buyers can like your solution and still lack a coherent interpretation of their own situation. When that happens, they cannot move forward internally because they do not know what they are actually advocating for.

2) Align: "Can we agree on what's true?"

Once the buyer has an interpretation, they have to share it.

This is where modern buying becomes political and cross-functional. With an average of thirteen stakeholders involved, alignment is not a side task; it is the center of the decision.[12]

Alignment fails in predictable ways:

- Stakeholders agree on symptoms but disagree on cause.
- Departments use different language for the same friction.
- Teams prioritize different outcomes and measure value differently.
- People resist publicly, even if they agree privately, because the timing feels unsafe.

When alignment fails, the deal does not "lose." It becomes too risky to advance.

3) Defend: "Can we justify this under scrutiny?"

Even when stakeholders align, the buyer must still defend the decision upward.

---

12. Forrester, "Buying Committees Have 13 Stakeholders," 2024 – an average of 13 people are involved in a buying decision; 89% of purchases involve two or more departments.

This is where "no decision" often happens. HBR's research shows how common it is for intent to exist without action. The buyer wants to move, but they cannot produce a defensible narrative that survives leadership scrutiny, budget review, and the internal politics of ownership.

In regret-heavy environments, this pressure multiplies. Gartner's findings on buyer regret explain why: buyers expect second-guessing and consequences, so they look for decisions that feel stable enough to defend later.

To move forward, the buyer must clearly articulate:

- Why now (not next quarter)
- Why this approach (not internal alternative)
- Why this investment (given limited resources)
- Why this solution (given political exposure)

When defendability fails, the deal collapses in rooms you never see.

1.6 Why This Chapter Matters (and What Comes Next)

Sales progress is *not* determined by what happens in your meeting. It is determined by what happens **after** your meeting—inside the buyer's internal world.

When you understand the Internal Buyer Journey, you can:

- Guide conversations with greater precision
- Reduce internal confusion and friction
- Help buyers build alignment that survives scrutiny
- Equip champions to win the internal sale
- Create momentum that continues without you

This journey is not linear. It is **ongoing, circular, and politically real**—and you will use it throughout the entire Buyer Sense Conversations Flow.

At this point, the pattern should be clear: buyers do not stall because your solution is unclear. They stall because their environment is.

Chapter 1 has one message: modern buying stalls are mostly internal.

- Buyers have limited time with vendors.
- Buyers encounter abundant high-quality information and still struggle to turn it into clarity.
- Buying groups are large and cross-functional.
- "No decision" is a primary outcome.
- Regret is common, which makes defensibility the dominant buyer instinct.

When founders miss this internal reality, they tend to respond with outward effort. They provide more information. They add pressure. They speed up. They push harder.

That response makes sense from the founder's perspective. It often increases friction from the buyer's perspective, because it adds force without reducing uncertainty.

So the next question becomes unavoidable: *What are founders doing—often unintentionally—that increases uncertainty instead of reducing it?* That is chapter 2.

WHAT FOUNDERS GET WRONG (AND WHY)

2.1 Why Founders Struggle with Sales

Most founders assume they struggle with sales because they're "not natural sellers." But that's not what's really happening. The problem isn't you. The problem is the **game you've been asked to play**.

The traditional sales playbook was built for a different species of seller: people working inside large organizations, backed by brand recognition, marketing engines, SDR teams, customer references, and a clear solution category. When those sellers show up, the room already knows roughly who they are and what they do. The system speaks for them before they say a word.

Founders walk into a completely different environment.

You are often:

- Introducing a new category or a strange-looking variant of an old one
- Unknown to the market
- Unproven in the eyes of the buyer
- Operating without case studies, logos, or internal champions

Yet you're trying to use the same playbook as the big vendors. No wonder it feels off. Founders don't struggle with sales because they lack charisma. They struggle because they're solving **a harder problem** with **the wrong template**.

The result is a predictable set of friction points—mistakes that don't feel like "mistakes" in the moment because they come from good instincts: enthusiasm, problem obsession, and a desire to help. But inside a modern buying environment, those instincts can unintentionally increase risk for the buyer.

2.2 The Seven Founder Mistakes That Increase Buyer Instability

2.2.1 You see the system, while buyers only see symptoms.[13]

As a founder, you've spent months—or years—inside the problem. You've seen the upstream causes, the downstream consequences, and the invisible patterns that connect them. Your brain is wired to think in systems.

Buyers rarely live at that altitude. They experience symptoms:

- "Reports are late."
- "Work keeps falling between teams."
- "Incidents keep reappearing."

When you describe the full system too quickly, you're not wrong—you're just too far ahead. The buyer feels like they're being dragged into a world they don't fully understand yet. And when people feel outpaced, their instinct is to slow down, ask for more time, or retreat into safe generalities.

This is where founders misread the moment. They assume the buyer is resisting the truth. More often, the buyer is resisting the

---

13. McKinsey, "The New B2B Growth Equation," 2021 – buying groups include 6–11 stakeholders with conflicting interpretations.

cognitive leap. They haven't built the internal map yet, so your deeper framing lands as complexity instead of clarity.

Founder Story: Jon Discovers the Real Problem

Jon was building an automation platform designed to eliminate manual work across operations teams. In conversations, buyers consistently agreed that automation was needed. They nodded when Jon explained the architecture. They liked the roadmap. Yet almost every deal stalled after the second or third call.

Buyers would say things like, "This makes sense," or, "We just need to think about how this fits," and then go quiet.

At first, Jon assumed resistance. He doubled down on explaining the system—how upstream data flowed, how dependencies were resolved, how automation reduced error rates across the entire workflow. The more clearly he explained the system, the more hesitant buyers became.

What Jon eventually realized was simple but uncomfortable: buyers were not struggling with automation. They were struggling with data reliability.

Operations leaders were living with inconsistent inputs that made automation feel dangerous. If the data failed, the automation would fail, and they would be blamed. When Jon framed everything around the full system too early, buyers felt pulled into a level of complexity they had not yet stabilized internally.

Once Jon slowed down and focused first on the symptom buyers recognized—unpredictable throughput—conversations changed. Not because the system was different, but because the buyer could finally see how it related to their issues.

Three deals that had stalled for months closed within thirty days. Nothing changed in the product. What changed was the starting point.

2.2.2 You compress years of insight into minutes.

Founders care deeply. That's the blessing and the trap. Because you've invested so much energy into your product, you feel a subtle pressure to "get it all on the table" in one conversation—every use case, every edge case, every clever capability. It comes from a good place: you want the buyer to see the full potential.

But cognitively, that conversation is too dense.[14] You're asking the buyer to process:

- A new problem frame
- A new solution
- New terminology
- New internal implications

And this is all in a forty-five- to sixty-minute slot squeezed between their real job. When processing demand exceeds mental capacity, people don't just lose details—they lose **confidence**. And when confidence drops, decisions slow, no matter how good your idea is. The buyer may still like you and still believe the solution has promise, but they leave the meeting without the one thing required for progress: a clean, stable understanding they can carry into their internal world.

Founder Story: Alex Learns to Slow Down

Alex had built a sophisticated project management platform with advanced forecasting, dependency tracking, and reporting logic. In early sales calls, he tried to do justice to everything the product could do.

He moved fast. He explained context. He showed workflows. He answered questions before buyers finished asking them. The calls felt productive. Buyers were polite and engaged.

---

14. MIT *Sloan Review*, "When Coordination Fails," 2019 – most operational problems originate from upstream system flaws, not local symptoms.

And then they disappeared.

Alex couldn't understand it. The value was obvious to him. The logic was sound. The product worked.

What Alex didn't see was the cognitive load he was creating. Buyers were being asked to absorb a new way of thinking about work, a new set of concepts, and a new internal implication—all in under an hour. They left the meeting impressed, but mentally saturated.

One buyer finally said it out loud after a long pause: "I like this, but I'm not sure how to explain it to my team yet."

That one sentence changed how Alex saw it. The problem wasn't that people weren't interested. It was that they couldn't carry it forward.

When Alex began slowing the conversation and focusing on one bottleneck, one pressure point, one consequence at a time, buyers stopped nodding politely and started asking better questions. The next calls didn't move faster. But the deals did.

2.2.3 You jump to solutions because you genuinely want to help.

Founders are builders. You see a problem and your instinct is to fix it. So in sales conversations, you often jump to:

- "Here's how we'd solve that."
- "Let me show you the workflow."
- "I can demo that part right now."

From your perspective, this is generosity. From the buyer's perspective, it can feel like **being moved too fast**. When someone is still trying to interpret their situation, an early solution can land as pressure: "They're already trying to sell me something, and I'm not even sure how to explain this internally yet."

The result isn't rejection. It's a polite delay. The buyer doesn't say no. They say, "Interesting," "Send me info," "Let's circle back," or, "We need to align internally."

That delay is not a stall caused by a lack of value. It's a stall caused by a lack of interpretability.

Founder Story: Emma Moves Too Fast

Emma was the founder of a customer analytics startup. In her mind, the problem was clear: teams lacked visibility into customer behavior across channels. So when buyers described pain—missed signals, reactive decisions, churn surprises—Emma immediately showed how her platform solved it.

She demoed dashboards. She walked through alerts. She explained how quickly insights surfaced.

Buyers responded with interest, but also hesitation. "We need to think about this internally." "Let us review this with the team."

Emma thought she was being helpful. Buyers felt rushed.

In hindsight, she realized that buyers were still trying to understand *what problem they were accountable for*. Was it churn? Visibility? Alignment between marketing and product? By presenting a solution before that question was settled, Emma unintentionally forced buyers to defend something they had not yet named.

The demos didn't push buyers away. They froze them.

When Emma later shifted her focus to understanding how buyers described the problem internally—before ever showing the product—conversations slowed down. But momentum returned.

2.2.4 You expect logic, while buyers bring overload.

Founders often come into the conversation with a clear narrative in mind: Problem → Impact → Solution → Next Step. But the buyer walks in carrying:

- Incomplete information from internal conversations
- Political pressure from above
- Competing priorities across teams
- Fear of being blamed if this goes wrong

You're speaking to them as if they're operating in a calm, rational state, but they're actually operating in a **fog**. In foggy conditions, even good ideas feel risky. People don't move forward on what is "best." They move forward on what feels safe to defend. And when safety is missing, they default to the safest option of all: **later**.

Founder Story: Daniel Talks to a Foggy Room

Daniel was selling a data governance platform to a large services organization. He entered the conversation prepared. He had a clear storyline, strong use cases, and a logical progression from problem to solution.

Within ten minutes, he could tell something was off.

The buyer kept interrupting—not with objections, but to add context to their situation:

- "We're also dealing with a reorg."
- "Security is pushing something similar."
- "This isn't my only priority right now."

Daniel tried to pull the conversation back to logic. He clarified the benefits. He re-explained the value. He tightened the narrative.

The buyer nodded politely but kept glancing at the clock.

After the call, Daniel felt frustrated. The logic was sound, and the need was real. Why wasn't it landing?

Only later did he realize that the buyer hadn't walked into the meeting ready to *evaluate*. They'd walked in carrying unresolved conversations, political pressure, and competing deadlines. The conversation didn't fail because the logic was weak. It failed because the buyer's mental bandwidth was already exhausted.

What Daniel experienced as *indifference* was actually *overload*.

2.2.5 You feel urgency, while buyers feel exposure.

You're building a company. Every conversation, every quarter, every lost deal matters. Your urgency is real. But inside the buyer's world, the emotional equation is different:

- You see opportunity.
- They feel exposure.

Saying yes means:

- Sponsoring a new initiative
- Asking others to change how they work
- Tying their name to something that might not land well

This is why founders often feel "push-pull" energy in deals that appear positive. The buyer may like the idea, respect the founder, and even want the outcome—yet still hesitate.

That hesitation is rarely about your product. It's about the cost of being wrong.

The emotional gap—your urgency versus their risk—creates invisible friction. When you push from urgency, they pull back from self-protection.

Founder Story: Sophie Pushes at the Wrong Moment

Sophie was running low on runway. Every deal mattered. When a procurement lead expressed interest in her compliance platform, Sophie leaned in.

She followed up quickly. She proposed timelines. She emphasized momentum:

- "If we want this live by Q3, we need to move soon."
- "Other teams are already looking at this."
- "This is the window to act."

From Sophie's perspective, this was responsible leadership.

From the buyer's perspective, it felt dangerous.

The procurement lead didn't object. Instead, they slowed the process:

- More internal reviews
- More stakeholders
- Longer gaps between responses

Eventually, the deal went quiet.

Only later did Sophie understand the dynamic. For the buyer, saying yes didn't mean purchasing software. It meant:

- Taking ownership of compliance risk
- Defending the decision across legal and security
- Being accountable if something went wrong

Sophie was pushing for speed. The buyer was managing personal exposure.

The urgency that felt necessary to Sophie made the decision feel unsafe to the buyer. And when safety disappears, progress does too.

2.2.6 You talk to one person. The decision belongs to many.

Most founder conversations start with a single motivated contact. It's easy to mistake that person for "the buyer." But in complex B2B environments, the real decision lives in a **web of**

stakeholders—finance, IT, security, operations, leadership, and sometimes legal or risk.

If your conversations never go beyond the first person, you're leaving the real arena untouched. The deal doesn't die because your contact changed their mind. It dies when they try to carry a half-formed story into a room full of people you've never met.

Without a shared narrative, the safest group decision is no decision.

This is also why founders get blindsided. They interpret the conversation as "a good call." Then they hear nothing. What happened is not ghosting. What happened is internal collapse: the story could not survive translation.

Founder Story: Lina Walks Into the Room She Wasn't In

Lina was selling a workforce optimization tool into mid-sized manufacturing firms. Her main contact was enthusiastic—a senior operations manager who clearly felt the pain and wanted change.

Every call went well. The contact agreed with the logic. He liked the approach. He promised to socialize it internally.

Then silence.

Eventually, Lina was invited to a broader meeting with finance, HR, and plant leadership. Within minutes, she saw the real problem. Finance was worried about cost variability. HR was concerned about labor relations. Plant leadership feared disruption during peak cycles.

None of this had come up in the earlier calls.

Lina realized the issue wasn't her champion's intent. It was the absence of a shared narrative strong enough to survive internal scrutiny. Her contact wasn't resisting. He was overwhelmed.

The deal hadn't stalled because the solution was weak. It stalled because the internal conversation had collapsed without her ever seeing it.

2.2.7 You have no brand to lean on—only clarity.

When a well-known vendor walks into the room, the buyer already trusts:

- The logo
- The category
- The general track record

That doesn't guarantee a win, but it lowers the perceived risk.

As a founder, you don't have that. You cannot borrow safety from your brand.

You have to create safety in the conversation itself.

You do that not with pressure, slickness, or perfect pitches—but with clarity about what the buyer needs to stabilize internally:

- What the problem really is (and what it is not)
- What is at stake if nothing changes
- What trade-offs exist (and why they matter)
- What internal risks and politics will shape the decision

This is why traditional sales advice often feels wrong on you. It asks you to perform. But performance doesn't reduce risk for modern buyers.

Clarity does.

Founder Story: Mark Competes Without a Logo

Mark was competing against a well-known enterprise vendor. On paper, his product was faster, simpler, and more flexible. Buyers agreed.

But when decisions approached, the familiar name always felt safer.

Mark couldn't offer brand reassurance. What he could offer was something else: clarity. He began spending less time explaining what his product did and more time clarifying what would happen if the buyer *did nothing*—where friction would increase, where costs would compound, where risks would quietly grow.

He didn't attack competitors. He helped buyers articulate trade-offs they were already living with.

Over time, buyers stopped comparing logos and started comparing consequences. Mark didn't win every deal. But when he won, it was because the buyer felt able to defend the decision—not because the product was flashy, but because the story made sense.

2.3 The Pattern Beneath Every Founder Mistake

At first glance, these mistakes appear different. Some founders overwhelm buyers with detail. Others move too fast. Others hesitate to challenge. Others push urgency. But beneath the surface, they all point to the same underlying failure.

Founders unintentionally increase the buyer's internal instability.

These mistakes do not kill deals through open rejection. They kill deals by making the decision harder to carry internally. Buyers do not walk away because they disagree with the solution. They pause because they cannot yet explain it, defend it, or align others around it.

This is why modern deal failure often feels ambiguous. The buyer stays engaged. The tone remains positive. Meetings continue. Yet progress slows or stops entirely.

Inside the buyer's organization, enthusiasm is not enough.

For a decision to move forward, it must survive internal scrutiny. It must make sense to people who were not part of the original conversation. It must withstand political pressure, competing priorities, and the personal risk attached to sponsorship. When founders leave buyers with fragments of insight but no coherent narrative, the safest internal move is delay.

Modern buying is not a moment of choice. It is a process of internal translation.

And translation fails when clarity is missing.

2.4 Why Effort Makes Things Worse Under Pressure

When founders sense hesitation, they often respond by doing more. More explanation. More justification. More urgency. More follow-up. These reactions are understandable, as they come from commitment and responsibility. But in complex buying environments, they often intensify the very problem they are trying to solve.

More information does not reduce uncertainty when the buyer does not yet know how to interpret it. More urgency does not accelerate decisions when the buyer feels exposed. More persuasion does not create confidence when the internal system is misaligned.

Instead, these moves increase cognitive and political load.

Buyers experience this as pressure — not because the founder is aggressive, but because the decision still feels unsafe. The result is polite resistance: requests for time, requests for material, requests for alignment. None of these signals mean "no." They mean, "I cannot carry this forward yet."

This is the moment where traditional selling logic breaks down.

Pressure assumes readiness. Persuasion assumes clarity. But most buyers are still trying to understand what they are deciding about.

2.5 The Blind Assumption at the Center of Founder Sales

All of the mistakes in this chapter trace back to one assumption founders rarely question:

Whether the buyer already has internal clarity.

In reality, buyers almost never do.

They may recognize symptoms, but not root causes. They may feel urgency, but not alignment. They may like the idea, but not yet see how it survives internal debate.

Founders step into conversations believing they are helping buyers evaluate a solution. Buyers are still trying to understand their situation well enough to take responsibility for changing it.

When this gap goes unrecognized, founders sell into instability. They add motion without direction. They create interest without safety. And they mistake activity for progress.

This is not a failure of intelligence or effort. It is a mismatch between how founders are taught to sell and how decisions actually move inside modern organizations.

Something different is required.

That shift from advancing a solution to stabilizing the decision environment is the pivot explored in chapter 3.

THE PIVOT – SENSEMAKING AND THE FOUNDER ADVANTAGE

3.1 Introducing Sensemaking (What It Is and What It Is Not)

The word *sensemaking* may sound abstract at first, but the experience it describes is deeply familiar to anyone who has ever tried to make a decision under pressure.

Sensemaking is the process by which people create clarity in situations that feel ambiguous, overloaded, or politically risky. It describes how humans move from confusion to meaning—not by receiving more information, but by interpreting what already exists in a way that holds together.

The concept was formally introduced into organizational research by Karl E. Weick in *Sensemaking in Organizations*.[15] Weick showed that in complex environments, people do not first understand and then act. They act in order to understand. Meaning emerges through interpretation, conversation, and shared framing, not through explanation alone.

This distinction matters deeply in modern B2B buying.

---

15. Karl E. Weick, *Sensemaking in Organizations* (Thousand Oaks, CA: Sage Publications, 1995).

Buyers today are not short on data, opinions, or options. They are surrounded by them. What they lack is a stable way to interpret their situation—one that makes sense across teams, survives internal scrutiny, and feels safe to stand behind. Sensemaking addresses that gap.

It is not about teaching buyers something new. It is about helping them more clearly see what they already live.

What Sensemaking *Is*

In the context of buyer conversations, sensemaking is the act of stabilizing meaning before pushing for action.

It helps buyers:

- Interpret what their symptoms actually point to
- Connect fragmented inputs into a coherent picture
- Align internal stakeholders around a shared understanding
- Reduce emotional and political risk attached to a decision

Sensemaking does not accelerate decisions by adding pressure. It accelerates decisions by removing confusion.

When sensemaking is present, buyers experience relief. They feel less alone with the problem. They gain language they can reuse internally. The situation stops feeling chaotic and starts feeling navigable.

This is why sensemaking often feels subtle from the outside. There is no dramatic pitch moment. No hard close. No performance. Instead, there is a noticeable shift in the buyer's posture—from guarded to engaged, from overwhelmed to thoughtful, from hesitant to grounded.

That shift is not persuasion at work. It is clarity taking hold.

What Sensemaking *Is Not*

Because sensemaking is often misunderstood, it's important to be precise about what it is not.

Sensemaking is **not** education. You are not there to explain everything, train the buyer, or deliver a masterclass on your domain. In fact, excessive explanation often undermines sensemaking by increasing cognitive load.

Sensemaking is **not** consulting. You are not diagnosing for free or solving the buyer's entire problem on the call. You are helping them interpret their situation well enough to move forward responsibly.

Sensemaking is **not** therapy. You are not validating feelings for their own sake or avoiding tension. Sensemaking often involves naming uncomfortable truths—but doing so in a way that reduces threat rather than amplifying it.

And sensemaking is **not** soft selling. It is not passive, vague, or indirect. Done well, sensemaking is precise, challenging, and deeply focused. It simply challenges in a way the buyer can absorb.

Where traditional selling pushes toward an answer, sensemaking clarifies the question.

Why Sensemaking Reduces Load Instead of Adding It

Modern buyers operate under two kinds of pressure at once.

The first is cognitive: too much information, too many opinions, too many frameworks, too many inputs competing for attention.

The second is political: decisions must be justified upward, defended sideways, and carried personally. Every recommendation carries exposure.

Traditional selling adds to both pressures. It introduces more information and increases the emotional cost of being wrong.

Sensemaking does the opposite. It reduces cognitive load by simplifying the problem into a structure the buyer can hold. And it reduces political load by giving the buyer a narrative that makes sense beyond the original conversation.

This is why sensemaking does not feel like influence to the buyer. It feels like support.

This is not support in the emotional sense, but in the structural sense, helping the buyer feel better equipped to think, speak, and act inside their organization.

That is the condition under which decisions actually move.

In the sections that follow, you will see why this shift—from selling to sensemaking—is not a stylistic preference but a response to how modern decisions truly work. And you will see why founders, more than any other sellers, are uniquely equipped to do this well.

Founder Story: When Clarity Replaced Pitching

Anna was a first-time founder, deeply convinced that her product's value would be obvious once buyers saw it. The technology worked. The use cases were real. The market need was clear. So she did what most founders are taught to do: she moved quickly into demos.

She clicked through features. She explained workflows. She showed how efficiently everything fit together. Her calls were energetic, confident, and full of capability.

And yet, they rarely ended the way she expected.

Buyers looked thoughtful—but uncertain. They asked a few polite questions.
They said things like "This looks interesting," or, "We need to discuss this internally."

Then they disappeared.

At first, Anna assumed this was normal early-stage friction. She told herself she needed more proof points, tighter demos, stronger urgency. But the pattern didn't change.

Then, during one particularly quiet meeting, something different happened.

As the call was wrapping up, the CFO paused. He didn't criticize the product. He didn't question the value. Instead, he said something that stopped Anna cold:

"Your product seems great . . . but I still don't understand the problem clearly enough to pitch this internally."

That sentence changed everything.

Anna realized the issue wasn't her product. It was the conversation.

She had been adding clarity about *the solution* while the buyer was still confused about *the situation*. She wasn't helping buyers make sense of their own world. She was unintentionally increasing the burden they carried into internal discussions.

So she made a simple—but profound—shift.

She stopped trying to sell.

And she started guiding buyers through clarity.

Instead of leading with features, Anna began opening conversations by mapping the buyer's environment: their pressures, their workflows, their internal dynamics, and what "good" actually meant inside their organization.

She asked fewer leading questions and more interpretive ones. She slowed the conversation down—not to delay progress, but to stabilize understanding. She focused less on what the product could do and more on what the buyer was accountable for explaining internally.

Within weeks, the tone of her conversations changed.

Buyers leaned in. They spoke more openly. They began inviting other stakeholders into the room.

Momentum returned—not because Anna became more persuasive, but because buyers felt safer. They could finally see the problem clearly enough to carry it forward.

Her close rate doubled.

Not because she changed the product. Not because she refined the pitch deck.
But because she changed how buyers experienced the decision.

What Anna discovered—without yet having a name for it—is the core shift this chapter is about: when clarity replaces pitching, decisions begin to move.

3.2 Why Traditional Selling Fails Modern Buyers

Traditional selling struggles today not because sellers lack skill or buyers lack intelligence, but because the underlying assumptions about how decisions are made no longer match reality. Most sales methodologies still operate as if buyers arrive with stable priorities, clear problem definitions, and the cognitive bandwidth required to evaluate options rationally. In modern B2B environments, none of these conditions reliably exist.

Research across Gartner, CEB, and McKinsey consistently shows that buyers struggle far more with internal alignment, problem definition, and risk interpretation than with distinguishing one vendor from another. When sellers respond to hesitation by adding more explanation, more features, or more persuasive logic, they unintentionally magnify the very overload buyers are already trying to manage. What feels like helpful clarity to the seller often lands as additional cognitive noise to the buyer.

This breakdown originates from a deeper misconception embedded in traditional selling models: the belief that buyers operate with a coherent internal narrative—one clear problem, one shared priority, one agreed decision path. In reality, most B2B buyers navigate fragmented organizational environments shaped by competing initiatives, political constraints, legacy systems, and multiple stakeholders who interpret the same situation through entirely different lenses. When a seller pushes too hard or too fast in this context, they rarely encounter rational objections. Instead, they collide with unspoken emotional and organizational barriers: "*I don't know how to justify this internally.*" "*My team isn't aligned.*" "*If this goes wrong, I'm the one who pays the price.*"

Across modern buying research, three forces appear repeatedly—and together explain why persuasion fails even when value is clear.

First, information overload. Gartner reports that 77% of B2B buyers describe the buying journey as "very complex or difficult," largely because every stakeholder brings different inputs, tools, opinions, and priorities into the process. Traditional selling responds to this complexity by adding information—more decks, more detail, more comparison—rather than helping buyers reduce and organize it. In overloaded systems, additional information does not increase confidence; it increases friction.

Second, interpretation gaps. CEB identified what they call the "interpretation problem": buyers often understand the facts but cannot extract meaning, priority, or internal relevance from them. Feature-heavy pitches widen this gap by providing data without context and solutions without shared problem definition. Buyers leave conversations informed but still uncertain how to frame the issue internally, which makes forward movement politically and psychologically risky.

Third, fear-weighted decision-making. Research from Harvard Business Review and Prospect Theory demonstrates that buyers overweight potential losses by a factor of two to three compared to equivalent gains, particularly under conditions of scrutiny and accountability. When sellers increase pressure in this psychological state—by accelerating timelines, emphasizing urgency, or pushing commitment—fear intensifies, certainty drops, and action becomes less likely. The safest choice becomes delay.

This is why traditional selling, no matter how polished, consistently underperforms in modern buying environments. It attempts to force movement in systems that are already overloaded, politically fragile, and psychologically stretched. It accelerates persuasion at the exact moment buyers need help interpreting what is happening around them. It mistakes engagement for readiness and enthusiasm for internal safety.

Sensemaking succeeds where persuasion fails because it aligns with how decisions actually unfold inside organizations today. It slows the moment not to delay progress, but to restore coherence. It helps buyers articulate what they are experiencing but cannot yet name. It reduces cognitive and political load by creating shared understanding before commitment is required. And most importantly, it transforms the decision from something that feels risky and exposed into something that feels structured, navigable, and defensible.

In environments defined by overload, persuasion feels like pressure. Clarity—real, grounded, shared clarity—feels like relief.

Buyer Psychology:
Pressure activates resistance. Clarity activates progress.

3.3 Sensemaking vs. Selling: A Fundamental Shift

The difference between selling and sensemaking is not a matter of tone or technique. It is a difference in orientation—toward the decision itself.

Traditional selling is designed to move buyers toward an answer. It assumes the question is already known, the problem already defined, and the decision environment already stable enough to support evaluation. From that starting point, the seller's role is to persuade: to present advantages, justify value, handle objections, and guide the buyer toward a preferred outcome.

Sensemaking begins from a different premise entirely. It recognizes that in modern B2B environments, the buyer is often unclear about the question itself. What appears to be hesitation is frequently not resistance to a solution, but uncertainty about how to interpret the situation, how to align internally, and how to defend any course of action once scrutiny begins. In this context, persuasion does not accelerate progress—it destabilizes it.

Selling attempts to reduce uncertainty by supplying answers. Sensemaking reduces uncertainty by helping buyers see their situation more clearly.

This distinction matters because clarity and conviction are not created in the same way. A buyer can be convinced by an argument and still feel unable to move. They can agree with a recommendation and still hesitate to sponsor it. They can believe in a product's value and still delay because the internal consequences of action remain undefined. Selling addresses agreement. Sensemaking addresses readiness.

Where selling asks, "*Why us?*" Sensemaking asks, "*What is really happening here?*"

Where selling emphasizes differentiation, proof, and urgency, sensemaking emphasizes interpretation, prioritization, and internal coherence. It helps buyers connect symptoms to causes, isolate what truly matters from what merely feels loud, and understand the trade-offs already embedded in their system. This is why sensemaking often feels slower at the surface but produces faster outcomes in reality: it stabilizes the decision environment before momentum is applied.

To buyers operating under overload, clarity is not neutral. It is emotionally relieving. When a founder helps a buyer articulate a problem in a way that feels accurate, shared, and defensible, tension drops. Conversations feel easier. Resistance softens—not because the buyer has been persuaded, but because they feel less exposed. The decision begins to feel manageable.

This is also why sensemaking is frequently misread as "soft" selling. It does not push. It does not rush. It does not dominate the conversation. But beneath that calm surface, something decisive is happening: the buyer's internal narrative is becoming more stable. Stakeholders can align. Risks can be named without triggering fear. Responsibility begins to feel containable rather than dangerous.

Selling tries to create movement by applying force. Sensemaking creates movement by removing friction.

The shift is subtle but profound. Founders who adopt sensemaking stop measuring progress by how compelling their pitch sounds and start measuring it by how clearly the buyer can explain the problem to someone else. They listen for different signals: not enthusiasm, but coherence; not agreement, but alignment; not urgency, but confidence.

This is why buyers often describe sensemaking conversations as "helpful" in a way they struggle to articulate. They do not feel sold to. They feel understood. And understanding—particularly under conditions of complexity and risk—is the foundation upon which all durable decisions are built.

Selling aims to win the conversation. Sensemaking aims to stabilize the decision.

Once that stability exists, selling becomes easier—not because the founder has learned a better pitch, but because the buyer is finally ready to hear one.

3.4 Founder Psychology: Why You Are Built for Sensemaking

Founders are rarely trained as salespeople, yet they often outperform traditional sellers once the conversation shifts away from pitching and toward clarity. This is not a coincidence, and it is not a personality quirk. It is the natural outcome of how founders think, how they learn, and how they solve problems.

Founders are builders first. Long before you ever tried to sell your product, you spent months—or years—living inside a problem. You observed where systems broke, where work slowed down, where people compensated manually, and where small inconsistencies created outsized consequences. This experience trains you to see structure where others see noise. You do not experience problems as isolated complaints; you instinctively look for upstream causes, downstream effects, and the invisible dependencies that connect them.

This systems-level orientation is precisely what overwhelmed buyers lack. When a buyer describes a symptom, you naturally start tracing how that symptom fits into a larger pattern. What feels like intuition to you is, in fact, a rare cognitive skill: the ability to reveal order inside complexity. Sensemaking depends on this ability.

Founders also carry a depth of domain empathy that cannot be replicated through sales training alone. You built your company because you were close to the problem—close enough to feel its friction, urgency, or absurdity firsthand. As a result, when buyers speak imprecisely or struggle to articulate what feels wrong, you hear more than the words they choose. You hear the tension behind them. You recognize the frustration, the constraints, and the pressure shaping their experience.

This allows founders to name realities buyers often feel but cannot safely express. In high-stakes environments, this matters more than eloquence. Buyers do not need someone to impress them; they need someone who understands the weight they are carrying.

There is also a psychological dimension to this advantage. Founder profiles tend to cluster around traits that support sensemaking rather than performance selling.

These traits often look like liabilities in traditional sales environments, but they become decisive strengths in complex decision contexts:

- **High openness**, enabling curiosity, creativity, and the ability to imagine better systems
- **Comfort with ambiguity**, allowing unfinished thinking without premature closure
- **Tolerance for uncertainty**, which keeps conversations exploratory rather than performative
- **Awareness of decision fragility**, noticing what feels risky or "off" in a customer's decision — and where it could break later if left unaddressed

Founders notice patterns everywhere. You have heard the same problem described by different customers using different language. You have watched similar teams fail in similar ways. You have seen how small workflow gaps compound into strategic risks over time. Buyers live inside these patterns, but they cannot step outside them. You can. Sensemaking lives in that gap—between lived experience and clear interpretation.

Another underestimated founder strength is simplification. Founders spend their days translating complexity for different audiences: engineers, investors, early customers, partners, and skeptics. Over time, this builds an ability to explain complex systems without distorting them. In modern B2B environments, this is not a communication skill; it is a form of emotional safety. When buyers feel that complexity is being reduced rather than amplified, their defensiveness drops and their thinking opens.

Finally, founders challenge differently. You are not constrained by a script or driven by quota optics. You ask deeper questions because you care about solving the right problem, not just advancing a deal. When you challenge buyers, it does not feel like manipulation or pressure. It feels like commitment to accuracy. Buyers sense this immediately. They do not experience you as someone trying to win; they experience you as someone trying to help them understand.

This combination—systems thinking, domain empathy, pattern recognition, simplification, and respectful challenge—makes founders uniquely suited for sensemaking. These are not sales traits. They are leadership traits. And in environments where decisions feel risky and unclear, leadership is what buyers follow.

Founders are not at their best when they perform. They are at their best when they help others see.

Petra's Insight
Founders are most effective when they stop trying to persuade and start helping buyers understand what is actually happening inside their world.

3.5 Buyer Sense Conversations: From Insight to Structure

By this point, one thing should be clear: understanding buyer psychology is necessary, but it is not sufficient.

Many founders reach this insight intuitively. They sense that buyers are overloaded. They notice that pushing harder backfires. They feel that clarity, not persuasion, is what moves decisions forward. And yet, despite this awareness, their results remain inconsistent.

The reason is simple. Insight without structure collapses under pressure.

In real sales conversations, founders are juggling competing demands: time limits, stakeholder dynamics, emotional signals, product knowledge, and the ever-present fear of losing momentum. Even the most perceptive founder will default to old habits when the conversation becomes tense or ambiguous. Without a clear structure to rely on, intuition alone is not enough.

This is where Buyer Sense Conversations begins.

Buyer Sense Conversations is not a mindset shift or a set of principles. It is a **structured decision method** designed to help founders guide buyers through the specific cognitive and emotional transitions required for modern decisions to move forward.

The goal is not to make founders sound smarter or more persuasive. The goal is to make the decision itself more stable.

At its core, the framework is designed to help buyers do three things they struggle to do on their own:

- **Interpret** what is actually happening inside their system
- **Align** the people and priorities involved in the decision

- **Defend** the decision internally once it moves beyond the conversation

These three internal processes—Interpret, Align, Defend—are always present in complex B2B decisions, whether sellers acknowledge them or not. When they are unsupported, decisions stall. When they are stabilized, progress follows naturally.

What founders need, therefore, is not more confidence or better storytelling. They need a repeatable way to **stabilize these internal processes in real time**, inside real conversations, with real organizational constraints.

Buyer Sense Conversations provides that structure.

It translates the psychology you've explored in Part I into a practical conversational flow—one that helps founders slow the right moments, apply pressure only when it is safe, surface risk without triggering fear, and build clarity that survives internal scrutiny.

Importantly, this structure does not constrain founders. It protects them.

It gives you something to rely on when buyers hesitate. It prevents you from rushing when urgency rises. It helps you recognize when a deal is not stalled—but unstable.

In other words, it turns clarity into something you can provide, not just hope for.

In the next section, you'll see the full Buyer Sense Conversations model at a high level—the stages, the emotional shifts buyers experience, and the internal work happening beneath the surface of every decision.

Part II will then walk through each stage in detail, showing you how to apply the framework step by step—without pressure, without manipulation, and without reverting to old sales habits when things get uncomfortable.

For now, what matters is this:

You are not missing effort. You are missing structure.

And structure is what turns insight into momentum.

3.6 The Buyer Sense Conversations Model (High-Level Overview)

The Buyer Sense Conversations model provides a clear structure for something that is usually invisible: how decisions are done inside complex organizations.

Most founders experience sales as a sequence of meetings, calls, and follow-ups. Buyers experience something very different. For them, a "decision" is not a moment—it is a progression of internal shifts that must occur before action feels safe. The model exists to make those shifts visible and guidable.

At a high level, the model consists of three interconnected layers.

The **outer layer** represents the *conversation stages* the founder actively guides. These stages describe how the conversation evolves—from initial orientation, through meaning-making and reframing, toward prioritization and mobilization. They are not a script and they are not a funnel. They are directional moves that help the conversation mature without forcing it forward prematurely.

The **middle layer** reflects the *emotional states* buyers must experience for progress to feel safe. These include understanding, awareness, clarity, agreement, timing, internal action, and safety. Buyers do not advance simply because logic is sound. They advance when emotional conditions allow them to carry the decision forward without fear of exposure.

The **inner layer** captures the most critical—and most often ignored—part of modern buying: the buyer's internal cognitive work.

Every complex decision requires buyers to do three things:

- **Interpret** what is actually happening inside their system
- **Align** people, priorities, and perspectives around a shared understanding
- **Defend** the decision once it leaves the conversation and enters the organization

These processes are always present, whether founders acknowledge them or not. When they remain unstable, deals stall quietly. When they become coherent, decisions begin to move.

The power of the Buyer Sense Conversations model is not in adding steps or sophistication. It is in creating stability. Each conversation stage exists to support one or more of these internal processes at the right moment—before urgency, before persuasion, and before pressure distort judgment.

Importantly, this model does not ask founders to abandon their instincts. It gives those instincts a structure they can rely on when conversations become complex, political, or emotionally charged. It helps founders recognize *where* a decision is unstable, rather than assuming resistance or lack of interest.

This is why the model works even when buyers appear engaged, positive, and collaborative—yet progress is slow. The issue is rarely motivation. It is almost always internal coherence.

In Part II, you will walk through each stage of the Buyer Sense Conversations flow in detail. You will learn how to guide these transitions deliberately, how to recognize when a buyer is not ready to move, and how to stabilize decisions without pressure or performance.

For now, what matters is simply this:

Modern B2B decisions do not fail because founders lack value. They fail because buyers cannot yet interpret, align, and defend what they are being asked to change.

The Buyer Sense Conversations model exists to solve that problem—systematically.

The model below on figure 3 shows the full architecture at a glance: outer ring with seven stages you guide in conversation, middle ring with the emotional conditions buyers need to feel safe moving forward, and inner ring with the hidden internal cognitive work every buyer must complete—Interpret → Align → Defend—before a decision can survive inside an organization.

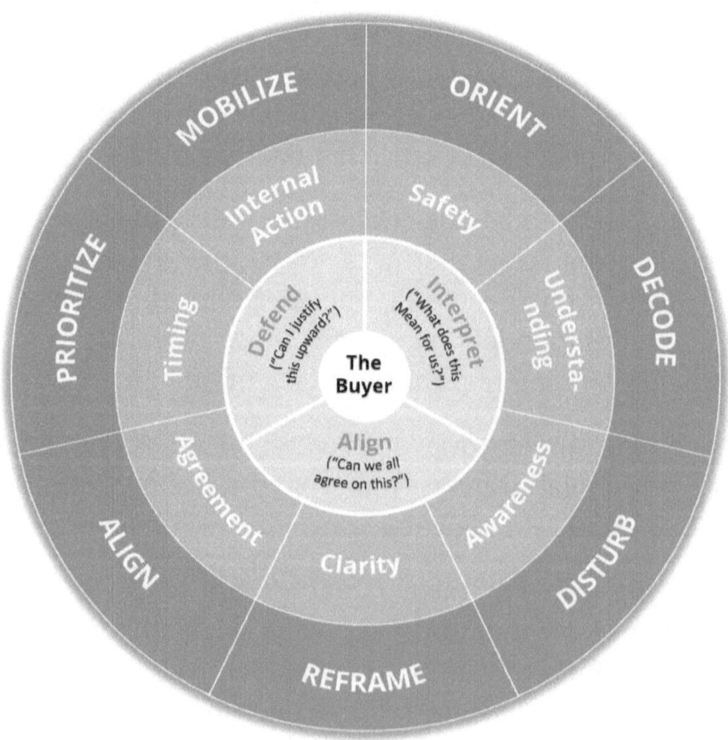

Figure 3: Buyer Sense Conversations

3.7 Why This Changes Everything (And What Comes Next)

What changes once you adopt sensemaking is not your personality or your pitch. What changes is what you are trying to move. Most founders try to move deals forward by increasing energy— more urgency, more follow-up, more explanation. Buyer Sense Conversations shifts the focus to something more foundational: stabilizing the decision environment so progress can actually hold.

When the buyer can interpret what is happening, align the people involved, and defend the decision internally, momentum stops being fragile. You no longer have to "manufacture" urgency. The system creates its own pull because the buyer can finally carry the decision without fear of being exposed.

This is why the method produces speed—just not the kind that comes from pressure. It produces the kind that comes from clarity.

To move decisions forward, founders must help buyers:

- Understand the *real* issue beneath the symptoms,
- Articulate what is true across teams,
- Create a narrative stakeholders can actually agree on,
- Build internal support before political resistance forms, and
- Navigate timing windows when organizational systems are receptive to change.

Modern B2B buying is not a product comparison. It is a **sensemaking challenge** happening inside the customer's walls. Your effectiveness depends on how well you guide it.

Part II is where we turn this into practice. You will learn the seven stages—Orient, Decode, Disturb, Reframe, Align, Prioritize, Mobilize—not as a script, but as a repeatable flow you can rely on in real conversations. You'll learn what to do when buyers hesitate, how to surface risk without triggering defensiveness, and how to build clarity that survives internal scrutiny.

You don't need to sell harder. You need to lead the decision.

Welcome to Part II.

THE SEVEN STAGES OF BUYER SENSE CONVERSATIONS™

(Orient → Decode → Disturb → Reframe → Align → Prioritize → Mobilize)

Part II gives you a practical, repeatable way to run Buyer Sense Conversations that turn buyer confusion into shared clarity, internal alignment, and confident next steps.

INTRODUCTION TO THE SEVEN STAGES

Now that you know the why, we'll talk about the how.

This chapter is where Buyer Sense Conversations moves from an idea to a usable system. Not a script you memorize, and not a set of "magic questions," but a repeatable structure you can run in real deals—especially the messy ones where stakeholders disagree, the buyer's story keeps shifting, and the next step feels strangely hard to name.

The Buyer Sense Conversations model is built to create forward motion without pushing. It helps you guide the buyer from scattered inputs to shared clarity: what's true, what's uncertain, what's actually blocking the decision, and what needs to happen internally for the buyer to move. The outcome isn't "a better pitch." The outcome is a decision that **makes sense inside the buyer's organization**—and a next step the buyer can take with **confidence.**

The strength of Buyer Sense Conversations lies not in persuading buyers to act, but in helping them interpret the terrain they must navigate: the unspoken risks, the hidden friction, the competing agendas, the technical and emotional inconsistencies that shape every decision. When you understand these forces, the conversation transforms. Buyers no longer see you as just a vendor. They see you as a provider of clarity in a landscape defined by noise.

Buyer Sense Conversations is built on a simple truth: buyers move forward when they experience **a sequence of emotional and cognitive shifts**, each one enabling the next. These shifts don't happen by accident. They are created by how you open the conversation, explore the buyer's world, name risks, reshape understanding, align stakeholders, clarify timing, and equip the champion to succeed internally.

This is not persuasion.

This is guidance.

This is leadership.

But clarity alone isn't enough. You need a way to **create** it—reliably, consistently, across different buyers and different organizations.

That is where structure comes in.

The system has seven stages: **Orient** → **Decode** → **Disturb** → **Reframe** → **Align** → **Prioritize** → **Mobilize**. Each stage has a specific purpose, a set of signals to listen for, and a clear output you're trying to produce. In the pages ahead, we'll walk through the full arc so you can see how the stages connect—and then we'll break them down one by one, so you can apply them immediately in your next conversation.

The Seven Stages at Glance

In Part I, you saw why modern buyers struggle: overloaded systems, political realities, and the constant fear of being wrong. Part II turns that understanding into structure. The seven stages of Buyer Sense Conversations give you a practical way to guide a buyer through that world—step by step, shift by shift—without feeling scripted or manipulative.

This section will show you:

- The psychology underneath each stage
- How modern buying really works behind the scenes
- Why founder-led conversations are different

- How the stages fit together into one coherent flow
- Where most founders unintentionally derail the process
- How to use this section in real calls, not just theory

Think of what follows as a **conversation map**: not a rigid script, but a structured way of thinking that keeps you aligned with how buyers actually make decisions.

The seven stages of Buyer Sense Conversations aren't random steps or a dressed-up sales funnel. They're a practical sequence you can run in almost any deal—because they map to the work that has to happen for a decision to become clear, aligned, and actionable.

Most conversations fail because they jump ahead. They push for "requirements" before the problem is fully defined, they pitch before the buyer can explain the situation internally, and they chase next steps before the stakeholders agree on what matters most. The seven stages prevent that by giving you a consistent order of operations—what to do first, what to establish next, and what "done" looks like at each step.

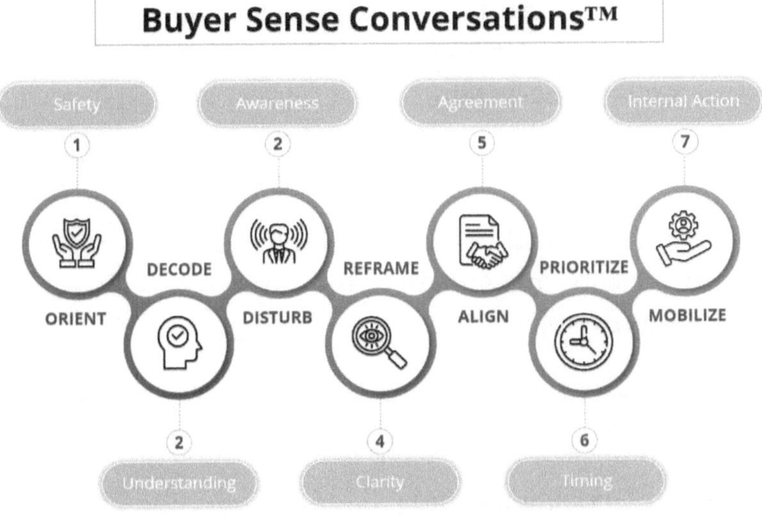

Figure 4: Buyer Sense Conversation

Here's the sequence:

Orient sets the context and the goal of the conversation.

Decode clarifies what's actually happening and what's driving the situation.

Disturb surfaces the cost of staying where they are and the risk of doing nothing.

Reframe simplifies the situation into a clear, usable way of understanding what's really going on.

Align turns that model into shared language stakeholders can repeat internally.

Prioritize defines what matters now versus later, and what must be true to proceed.

Mobilize converts clarity into a plan: next steps, internal actions, and decision movement.

When you use the stages this way, you don't rely on improvisation. You lead with structure, you keep the deal from skipping critical work, and you make progress measurable—stage by stage, conversation by conversation.

Why Buyer Sense Conversations Exists

We have already established that buyers are not looking for more information, but more clarity. That is why Buyer Sense Conversations exists:

They give founders a way to lead conversations that create:

- Deeper clarity about what is really going on
- Better thinking around risk, trade-offs, and priorities
- Alignment across teams and stakeholders
- Stronger, more defensible decisions

Your unfair advantage is not your product alone. It is how deeply you understand the buyer—and how well you can help them understand themselves.

How the Seven Stages Fit Together (Flow Map)

The seven stages of Buyer Sense Conversations are not tactics. They are a sequence of **mental transitions** the buyer must move through in order to understand, align on, and ultimately champion a decision. Each stage unlocks a specific emotional and cognitive state—one that becomes the foundation for the stage that follows. Skip a stage, and the entire structure collapses.

Modern decisions are fragile. They move forward only when the buyer feels safe, clear, aligned, and internally supported. This is why each stage matters:

1. **ORIENT → Safety:** Set a calm, buyer-led tone and define the purpose of the conversation so the buyer can think clearly instead of feeling managed.
2. **DECODE → Understanding:** Map what's happening in the buyer's world—systems, constraints, and friction—so the real problem becomes concrete.
3. **DISTURB → Awareness:** Surface the true cost of inaction and the risks of the status quo so the buyer can't unsee what's at stake.
4. **REFRAME → Clarity:** Offer a cleaner, simpler way to understand the situation that makes the path forward obvious and discussable.
5. **ALIGN → Agreement:** Turn individual clarity into shared language and stakeholder alignment so the decision doesn't die in internal meetings.
6. **PRIORITIZE → Timing:** Help the buyer decide what matters now versus later and identify the conditions and window for taking action.
7. **MOBILIZE → Internal Action:** Equip the buyer to drive the

next steps internally with a defensible narrative, evidence, and a clear plan.

Why Skipping a Stage Breaks the Deal

When founders jump ahead—often with the best intentions—they disrupt the psychological sequence buyers rely on. Skipping even one stage creates:

- **Friction**—because the buyer doesn't yet have the mental model needed to follow you
- **Mistrust**—because the conversation feels rushed or self-serving
- **Confusion**—because risks, priorities, or definitions remain unclear
- **Internal resistance**—because the buyer cannot champion a decision they don't fully understand

The flow map is not rigid. It is rhythmic. It reflects how real decisions move—from emotional grounding, to interpretation, to clarity, to alignment, to confident action.

When you honor this progression, conversations feel natural, buyers feel supported, and decisions move forward with far less friction.

How to Read This Section

The pages that follow are not designed to give you lines to memorize. They are designed to change how you **think** during a conversation.

Each stage will walk you through:

- The underlying psychology at play for the buyer
- The purpose of that stage in the overall flow
- Concrete examples and short dialogues
- Common founder mistakes to avoid

- Core questions that unlock insight
- Conversation patterns you can adapt to your style
- Simple tools and frameworks you can use in real deals

Treat this section less like a script library and more like a **navigation manual**. You will not use every question in every call. You will not move through each stage in a perfectly straight line. Real conversations breathe.

What matters is that you internalize the **mental shifts**:

- When does the buyer need safety?
- When do they need shared interpretation?
- When do they need awareness of risk?
- When do they need a clearer frame?
- When do they need help aligning others?
- When do they need timing clarity?
- When do they need support to act internally?

If you read the stages with these questions in mind, you'll start to feel the Flow instead of forcing it. The goal is not to sound like this book. The goal is to **think** like a sensemaker while sounding like yourself.

Follow the stages as internal checkpoints rather than rigid steps—and your conversations will begin to transform.

How to Use the Seven Stages in Real Calls

Many founders worry they need to memorize every question or execute each stage perfectly. You don't. Buyer Sense Conversations is not a rigid script. It is a **thinking system**—a way of guiding buyers through the mental transitions that allow them to understand their world more clearly.

Use the stages as orientation points, not performance markers. Real conversations move, bend, loop, and reveal themselves in unexpected order. Your job is simply to know where you are and what the buyer needs next.

Here's how to apply the stages in real calls.

If you remember only one thing: your job is not to move the conversation forward—it is to stabilize the buyer's decision. When momentum breaks, it is almost never because the buyer lacks interest. It is because one internal condition—clarity, alignment, safety, or defendability—has become unstable. Use the stages not as steps to perform, but as a way to diagnose what the buyer needs next.

1. You don't need every question

Each stage includes many possible questions, but in practice you will use only a handful—typically three to five. Choose the questions that help the buyer think, not the ones that make you sound polished. The right question is the one the buyer can answer honestly.

2. You can move forward or backward

Conversations are nonlinear. Buyers jump ahead, circle back, or reveal something critical late in the call. Your job is to recognize when the buyer has slipped out of a necessary mental state and guide them back.

- If the buyer seems lost → return to **Decode**
- If they minimize the issue → return to **Disturb**
- If teams disagree → return to **Align**
- If timing becomes vague → deepen **Prioritize**

Think like a navigator, not a presenter.

3. Never skip safety

Without psychological safety, buyers cannot tell the truth. They will hide political tension, downplay uncertainty, and give polite but useless answers.

Safety is not soft; it is structural. It determines whether the buyer is willing to explore risk, contradiction, or misalignment. That is why **Orient is the foundation of the entire system.** If safety is missing, nothing else can take root.

4. Don't manufacture urgency—reveal it

Traditional selling pushes urgency. Buyers interpret this as pressure and instinctively retreat. Prioritization must emerge from *their* understanding of consequences—not your insistence.

Help them see:

- What changes if nothing changes
- Where delays accumulate downstream
- Which opportunities narrow over time
- How risks compound quietly

When buyers understand the cost of waiting, urgency becomes self-evident.

5. Align before you advance

Misalignment is the silent killer of deals. No amount of ROI arguments or product demos can overcome a fragmented internal narrative. Before you talk solutions, ask: **"Who else needs to see this interpretation for this to move forward internally?"**

If alignment isn't present, momentum is an illusion.

6. Treat prioritization as clarity, not pressure

Asking, "Is this a priority?" forces buyers into a defensive posture. Instead, explore the rhythms of their organization:

- Planning cycles
- Budget gates
- Operational constraints
- Regulatory or seasonal windows
- Current bottlenecks

When you illuminate the environment, buyers discover priority naturally. Once constraints and timing are visible, urgency emerges on its own—no pushing required.

7. Remember: mobilization is where deals are won

The final decision is rarely made with you present. It happens in internal meetings—where champions must defend your solution to people who were never on your call.

Your job is to equip them with:

- A clear articulation of the problem
- A shared interpretation others can adopt
- Language for cross-functional alignment
- A defensible logic the organization can stand behind

A great call creates clarity. A great mobilization strategy creates decisions.

8. Clarity beats persuasion—every time

Across every stage, your work is to raise clarity about the following:

- The real problem
- Consequences
- Meaning
- Alignment
- Timing
- Internal narrative

When clarity increases, resistance falls. When resistance falls, momentum becomes natural.

9. Your job is not to impress—it's to interpret

Buyers don't need a charismatic pitch. They need someone who can help them understand what they've been sensing but haven't been able to articulate. When you give them language for their own world, trust accelerates instantly.

Final Note

The stages are the engine of the conversation. The questions are your tools. Your presence, calmness, and ability to interpret complexity are the fuel.

Master the shifts—not the script—and every conversation becomes easier.

FROM ORIENTATION TO MOBILIZATION: MASTERING THE SEVEN BUYER SENSE STAGES

What follows is a practical walkthrough of the seven stages as they appear in real buyer conversations. Not in theory, and not in ideal order—but as they unfold under pressure, uncertainty, and organizational complexity.

Each stage is explored through buyer psychology, real dialogue, common founder missteps, and clear signals for when the conversation is ready to move—or needs to stay where it is. The goal is not progression for its own sake, but stability: helping decisions form in a way buyers can carry forward, defend internally, and act on with confidence.

Read these stages less as steps to execute and more as lenses to recognize where the buyer actually is—and what the conversation truly needs next.

STAGE 1: ORIENT

1. Psychology of Orient

Most founders begin conversations by pitching because they assume the buyer needs to be impressed before the real dialogue can begin. In reality, buyers arrive at calls with the opposite expectation. They anticipate pressure, hidden agendas, or a thinly veiled attempt to steer them toward a solution they're not yet ready to consider. Their nervous system enters the meeting braced for evaluation rather than collaboration.

Orient exists to neutralize this state. Before a buyer can think clearly, explore nuance, or reveal internal friction, they must first feel safe. The human brain cannot engage in complex reasoning while monitoring for threat; it needs psychological space. Orient creates that space by shifting the buyer out of defensive vigilance and into a state of relaxed attention. It signals, immediately and implicitly, that this will not be another sales performance they must endure—it will be a conversation designed for them.

Psychologically, Orient has one essential purpose: to reduce perceived threat and increase the buyer's sense of control. When buyers feel in control of the conversation, their cognitive load decreases. When they feel understood, their willingness to share increases. When they feel safe, they stop performing and begin thinking. This is why Orient is the most critical stage in the entire Buyer Sense system. Without it, every other stage competes with the buyer's protective instincts.

A buyer who feels safe will tell you what is real. A buyer who feels pressured will tell you nothing.

2. Purpose of Orient

The purpose of Orient is to establish the emotional and cognitive foundation upon which the rest of the conversation depends. It creates an environment where the buyer feels they are entering a productive dialogue rather than a sales interaction. When done well, Orient communicates four things instantly: this conversation is safe, structured, tailored, and under the buyer's control.

Safety emerges when the buyer senses the absence of pressure. Understanding emerges when they recognize that you have prepared thoughtfully and are speaking to their world—not delivering a generic pitch. Control emerges when you set a clear structure for the conversation, allowing them to anticipate its flow rather than react defensively. Respect emerges when they see that you have invested effort before entering the call.

By the time Orient is complete, the buyer should feel a quiet, confident shift:
"This will be a useful and safe conversation."

3. What Great Sounds Like

A great Orient doesn't sound like a performance. It sounds like a calm, confident leader guiding a conversation with intention. You speak with ease and clarity, establishing the structure of the discussion without haste or apology. The tone is steady and non-reactive. The buyer relaxes as they realize they are not being rushed into evaluation. Their answers lengthen, their posture softens, and their attention sharpens.

What makes Orient powerful is not the content—it is the emotional signal it sends:
You are safe. This is your time. This is your conversation.

4. What Bad Sounds Like

A weak Orient reveals itself instantly. The founder speaks too quickly or dives prematurely into product details. The conversation lacks structure, leaving the buyer unsure of where it is headed. Questions feel generic rather than thoughtful. The founder apologizes, over-explains, or tries to justify their presence. The buyer responds with guarded, minimal answers and keeps their emotional distance.

Most calls that feel "off" never recover from a poor Orient. The opening minutes set the entire trajectory.

5. The Three Jobs of Orient

Although Orient lasts only a short portion of the conversation, it performs three foundational jobs.

The first is establishing psychological safety. Until the buyer's defensive instincts settle, their mind remains in evaluation mode rather than exploration mode. Orient signals that you are not here to pressure or perform, but to understand.

The second is setting the agenda. Clarity reduces cognitive strain. When buyers know exactly how the conversation will unfold, they can participate fully rather than brace for surprise.

The third is demonstrating preparedness. Buyers reward those who have clearly invested in understanding their context, priorities, or recent developments. This isn't about showing research—it's about sounding oriented. Preparedness communicates respect, and respect opens doors that persuasion never will.

Once these three jobs are accomplished, the dynamic between you and the buyer shifts decisively. The call becomes collaborative instead of adversarial.

6. Common Founder Mistakes in Orient

Founders lose more calls in the first ninety seconds than in any other moment. They start with product, ask vague questions, appear uncertain, or talk at length about themselves. They unintentionally create pressure where they meant to create connection. The result is always the same: guarded answers, limited insight, and a buyer who remains emotionally distant for the rest of the conversation.

7. Mini-Dialogue Example: Tom and the Safety-First Frame

The impact of Orient is easiest to see in the first minute of a real conversation. It is not about what is said, but about what changes in the buyer once safety and structure are established.

In the example below, notice how Tom does not react to the buyer's impatience or try to overcome it. Instead, he uses preparation, structure, and intent to shift the emotional tone of the conversation—creating the conditions for real dialogue before any selling occurs.

Tom: Before we dive in, I want to make sure this conversation is actually useful for you. We've got about twenty-five minutes—would it help if we spent the first part mapping how this currently works on your side, and then decide together whether it's worth going deeper?

VP: (slight pause) Sure. That would be helpful.

Tom: Great. I also noticed in your last quarterly update that throughput variability showed up as a concern—especially between Ops and Planning. I don't want to assume that's still the core issue though. From your perspective, what made now the right moment to have this conversation?

VP: Honestly? We're feeling more pressure from leadership. The misses are getting harder to explain.

Tom: That makes sense. Then let's focus on understanding what's creating that pressure and where it's actually coming from. If at any point this isn't useful, we'll adjust.

VP: Okay. That sounds good.

8. Core Orient Questions

The questions used in Orient are simple, but they serve a profound psychological purpose: they return control to the buyer.

They are not about logistics or qualification—they are about lowering threat and inviting collaboration.

- "What would make this conversation most useful for you today?"
- "What prompted the timing of this conversation right now?"
- "Would it be helpful if we structured the next [X] minutes together?"
- "Before we dive in, is there anything you want to make sure we cover?"
- "How would you like this conversation to be different from typical sales calls?"

Asking what would make the conversation useful, what internal factors prompted the timing, or whether a structured approach would help gives the buyer agency. These questions are not logistical; they are neurological. They lower the buyer's guard and invite them into co-authorship of the conversation.

9. Stage Transition: How You Know Orient Is Complete

You move to Decode only when the emotional tone of the conversation changes. The buyer agrees to the agenda. Their speech becomes less guarded. They begin volunteering meaningful details rather than rehearsed explanations. They speak from inside their world rather than from behind a protective shield.

This shift—from evaluation to collaboration—is your signal that Orient has done its job.

If these signals have not appeared, you stay in Orient. The cost of moving forward too soon is far greater than the cost of pausing.

10. Mastering Stage 1 – Orient

Reflect on how you open conversations today. Rewrite your Orient so it can be delivered confidently in under thirty seconds. Identify the physical and verbal cues that signal buyer tension—and decide how you will diffuse them. Prepare tailored agendas for different buyer personas. Think through how you will demonstrate preparation before the call even begins. Write the single sentence you want buyers to think at the end of your Orient.

To make this concrete, here's what strong Orient execution looks like in a few common scenarios.

Scenario 1: The Rushed Executive

Signal: Short answers, multitasking, checking the clock.

Orient focus: Control, respect for time, clear structure.

Example Orient: "Before we jump in, I want to be respectful of your time. We have twenty minutes. My thought was to spend ten understanding how this is showing up today, and then decide together if it's worth continuing. Does that work for you?"

Desired buyer thought: "This will be efficient and on my terms."

Scenario 2: The Skeptical Buyer

Signal: Guarded tone, arms crossed, neutral or dismissive language.

Orient focus: Safety, non-agenda-driven intent, relevance.

Example Orient: "I don't want to assume this is a priority for you.

What made you open to this conversation now—and what would make it genuinely useful from your perspective?"

Desired buyer thought: "I'm not being sold to. I'm being listened to."

Scenario 3: The Curious but Overloaded Team Lead

Signal: Verbose answers, jumping ahead, listing problems without structure.

Orient focus: Containment, clarity, cognitive relief.

Example Orient: "It sounds like there are several moving parts here. If it helps, we can slow this down and map what's actually happening first—then see what matters most to focus on today."

Desired buyer thought: "Finally—someone is helping me make sense of this."

Across all scenarios, the goal of Orient is the same: to reduce perceived threat, restore a sense of control, and create a clear container for the conversation. When you master Orient, you don't just start calls better. You change how buyers experience the entire decision.

Mastering these elements turns the opening moments of every conversation into a strategic advantage.

STAGE 2 – DECODE

1. Psychology of Decode

Buyers rarely describe their reality accurately. Not because they are hiding information, but because they experience their world through **symptoms**—the fires they put out, the delays they absorb, the recurring breakdowns they learn to normalize. When they speak, they describe the visible edges of the problem, not the system underneath it.

Decode is where the conversation moves beneath the surface. By this stage, the buyer's nervous system has softened thanks to Orient, allowing them to think more clearly. Yet even with that clarity, buyers still cannot interpret what actually drives the patterns they experience. They misdiagnose root causes, underestimate cross-team impact, and speak from their own vantage point rather than the system as a whole. They often avoid admitting internal issues because doing so feels politically risky.

Decode exists to illuminate the machinery beneath their symptoms. It uncovers the hidden dynamics—the upstream triggers, downstream consequences, and systemic constraints—that the buyer senses but cannot articulate.

Buyer psychology reveals a consistent truth: **Most buyers can tell you *what* is happening. Decode uncovers *why* it is happening.**

2. Purpose of Decode

The purpose of Decode is to build a full, coherent map of how the buyer's world actually functions. Not in theory, not on official process diagrams, but in lived reality. In this stage, you uncover how work flows, where friction originates, how it spreads, who absorbs it, and which constraints keep the entire issue in place.

Decode transforms vague narratives into structural understanding. It gives shape, causality, and sequence to what previously felt chaotic.

When Decode is done well, the buyer feels a profound shift: **"You understand our world even better than we do."** No case study or credential slide accelerates trust faster than this moment.

3. What Great Sounds Like

A strong Decode conversation feels more like a thoughtful systems assessment than a sales call. The tone is investigative but never intrusive, curious but never judgmental. You guide the buyer into describing how things actually work—not how they believe they work or how they wish they worked. You prompt them to walk you through flows, handoffs, and breakpoints. You connect dots softly, letting the buyer hear their own logic reflected back to them.

When Decode is conducted skillfully, buyers experience small realizations in real time: connections between teams, patterns they had overlooked, or consequences they had normalized. This is when the buyer begins to feel deeply understood.

4. What Bad Sounds Like

Decode collapses when founders revert to traditional discovery habits—generic questions, premature solution talk, or narrow focus on surface-level complaints. When founders interrogate rather than explore, buyers shut down. When founders accept symptoms at face value, the conversation remains shallow. When founders stay within one department's perspective and ignore cross-team dynamics, the real system remains hidden.

Poor Decode results in shallow answers, no new insight, and no foundation for the next stages.

5. Common Founder Mistakes in Decode

Founders often move too quickly, accepting the buyer's symptoms as the real problem. They forget that every visible issue has invisible origins. They shy away from asking for specifics out of fear of sounding probing. They avoid exploring cross-functional friction because it feels politically sensitive. They focus only on the buyer's department and miss the system-wide chain reactions. Or, eager to be helpful, they jump ahead to solutions before the architecture of the problem is understood.

These mistakes weaken every subsequent stage. A poor Decode makes strong Disturb impossible.

6. Business Reality: Where Decode Lives

Decode lives in the messy, unfiltered reality of how work actually gets done. It uncovers what never appears in slides: the shadow workflows, manual interventions, ownership gaps, and fragile handoffs that create systemic breakdowns. In real organizations, work rarely follows the clean sequence described in documentation. It flows across teams with unclear ownership. It depends on tools that should integrate but don't. It relies on people compensating for broken processes.

When you Decode effectively, you become the first person in the conversation capable of seeing the following:

- The full upstream-to-downstream chain of events
- Who actually absorbs the friction when something breaks
- Which structural constraints keep the pattern recurring

This is why Decode feels transformational to buyers.[16] For the first time, someone is describing their environment as they live it—not as it appears on a sanitized process map.

7. Mini-Dialogue Example: Following the Chain Reaction

The impact of Decode becomes visible once the buyer starts describing their reality beyond surface symptoms. This stage is not about extracting information, but about helping the buyer *see the system they are already living inside.*

In the example below, notice how the founder does not accept the first answer as the full explanation. Instead of diagnosing or offering solutions, they calmly follow how the issue propagates upstream and downstream—until the buyer hears the pattern forming in their own words.

Founder: Walk me through what happens the moment this issue shows up.

Supervisor: Operators step in manually, and QC usually gets delayed.

Founder: And when QC gets delayed, what tends to happen next?

Supervisor: Planning starts adjusting forecasts.

Founder: When planning adjusts the forecast, how does that affect scheduling?

Supervisor: Scheduling stops trusting the data. They start double-checking everything.

Founder: So, one manual intervention ends up breaking trust in the entire planning system.

---

16. Decode maps workflows/friction, mirroring Challenger Sale "tailor" where top 20% reps decode context 2.5x better, boosting relevance.

Supervisor: (pause) Yes. That's exactly what's happening.

This is Decode at work—not uncovering a new problem but making an existing chain reaction visible and undeniable.

8. Core Decode Questions

Use four to six of these questions per call, adapting them to your style and the buyer's situation.

How It Actually Unfolds

- "Walk me through what happens before this becomes a problem."
- "What usually sets this in motion on a normal day?"
- "Who's the first person or team that gets pulled in?"

How It Spreads

- "Once this starts, what does it tend to affect next?"
- "Who ends up dealing with the consequences, even if they weren't involved at the start?"

Where It Breaks Down Under Pressure

- "Which part of this is the least predictable?"
- "What slows everything down when things get busy or tense?"

These questions help buyers see the chain reaction they're already living inside—without feeling interrogated or pushed.

9. Stage Transition: How You Know Decode Is Complete

You move to DISTURB only when you have the complete upstream-to-downstream chain and the buyer recognizes its accuracy. You will hear them say, "Yes . . . that's exactly how it works." You will uncover at least one repeating pattern. The buyer's tone will shift from descriptive to reflective. They will begin asking, "Why does this keep happening?"

If those signals haven't appeared, Decode isn't finished.

10. Mastering Stage 2 – Decode

Decode is where founders either earn deep credibility—or quietly lose it. Your job here is not to collect answers, but to reveal how the buyer's world actually works beneath the surface symptoms.

Reflect on how you currently run discovery. Do you accept stated problems at face value, or do you trace them upstream and downstream until the real system becomes visible? Practice slowing the conversation down, following cause-and-effect chains, and staying curious long enough to uncover patterns the buyer has learned to normalize.

To make this concrete, here's what strong Decode execution looks like in a few common scenarios.

Scenario 1: The Symptom-Focused Buyer

Signal: The buyer describes the problem in isolated terms ("Engineering is slow." "Handoffs are messy." "Alerts are overwhelming.") without connecting it to the broader system.

Decode focus: Manifestation, sequence, causality, upstream triggers, downstream consequences.

Example Decode: "Let's walk this through step by step. When this shows up in day-to-day work, what happens first? And after that, who feels it next?"

Desired buyer thought: "I've never mapped it like this before— and now I can see what's actually driving it."

Scenario 2: The Politically Cautious Buyer

Signal: Vague language, careful wording, avoidance of ownership or cross-team friction.

Decode focus: Safety, neutrality, system-level framing rather than blame.

Example Decode: "When this breaks down, who usually has to step in to keep things moving—regardless of who officially owns it? And what does that do to their workload?"

Desired buyer thought: "They're helping me describe reality without putting me at risk."

Scenario 3: The Overconfident Diagnoser

Signal: The buyer quickly names the root cause and jumps toward solutions ("we just need more headcount," "we need better tooling," "this is a process issue").

Decode focus: Verification, pattern testing, reality checking—without confrontation.

Example Decode: "That might be part of it. Before we settle there, can we trace what tends to happen right before the problem shows up—and what reliably breaks afterward? I want to make sure we're solving the right layer."

Desired buyer thought: "Maybe the issue isn't where I thought it was."

Across all scenarios, the goal of Decode is the same: to replace assumptions with structure, opinions with patterns, and surface complaints with a shared understanding of how the system actually behaves.

When Decode is done well, buyers don't feel interrogated. They feel understood. They stop defending symptoms and start exploring causes. And for the first time, the real problem becomes discussable.

Mastering Decode turns discovery from a polite Q&A into a

moment of genuine clarity—one that everything else in the conversation depends on.

ADVANCED DECODE

*(For enterprise, multi-team, technical,
or politically complex environments)*

Why Decode Is the Real Discovery

Decode is not traditional discovery. Discovery uncovers what the buyer wants. Decode uncovers how the buyer's environment actually behaves. It reveals the hidden architecture of decisions: the interdependencies, constraints, handoffs, and political dynamics that shape behavior.

When founders understand the system, buyers feel understood in a way they rarely experience with vendors. This is where real credibility is built.

Buyer psychology consistently confirms: **Buyers trust the person who understands their world better than they do.**

Mapping Business Systems

Every organization operates inside a system that is far more fragile, interconnected, and political than it appears. Decode uncovers upstream inputs, downstream dependencies, owners of each step, predictable failure points, shadow processes, and cross-team misalignment—showing how small breakdowns propagate across the system. These elements explain why problems persist even when people work hard and care deeply.

When founders map these systems, they reveal hidden costs and structural friction no slide or metric could capture.

Revealing Hidden Friction

Every company has silent friction: manual rework, unclear handoffs, shadow workflows, decision bottlenecks, competing priorities, and tense cross-team dependencies. When you surface these gently, buyers often say: "We've never mapped it like that before."

This is one of the strongest trust-accelerating moments in enterprise sales.

Advanced Decode Questions

1. What upstream event reliably triggers this issue?
2. Who absorbs the downstream impact?
3. Where does predictability break first?
4. Which team feels the most pain?
5. What workarounds exist today that leadership doesn't see?
6. Whose priorities are in tension here?
7. What decisions consistently slow things down?
8. What does leadership underestimate about this process?
9. Who becomes the bottleneck under stress?
10. What gets escalated most frequently—and why?

Dialogue Example: Decode in Action (SaaS)

Graham: Walk me through how a feature moves from ideation to release.

Product manager: We use Jira. Engineering picks items up as they can.

Graham: Before a ticket reaches engineering, what needs to happen upstream?

Product manager: Sometimes the spec isn't clear, sometimes the design is late.

Graham: And when the requirements aren't clear, who ends up dealing with it downstream?

Engineering lead: We do. We rewrite it mid-sprint.

Graham: What does that do to predictability?

Engineering lead: Destroys it.

In five questions, the real issue emerges: upstream ambiguity, not engineering capacity.

Founder Story: How Decode Changed Everything for Maya

Maya is a founder navigating early enterprise sales.

Maya once relied on traditional discovery questions and received predictable results: polite interest and no urgency. When she shifted to Decode, everything changed.

She asked who owned incident response upstream and learned that Security rewrites half of Operations' work. She asked who suffers downstream delays and uncovered a web of impact across Finance, Legal, and PR. In seven minutes, she revealed cross-functional chaos no vendor had ever surfaced.

The CISO leaned back and said: "That's . . . uncomfortably accurate. You're seeing things most vendors completely miss."

Decode created urgency because it created clarity.

STAGE 3 – DISTURB

1. Psychology of Disturb

Disturb is the moment in the conversation where you introduce **constructive tension**—not to frighten the buyer, but to help them see their situation with renewed clarity. It looks, on the surface, as if you are pointing out risks and friction. At a deeper psychological level, you are guiding the buyer through a necessary update of their mental model.

Organizations are remarkably good at normalizing dysfunction. Teams adapt to broken workflows, unreliable systems, political bottlenecks, and chronic rework until the true cost becomes invisible. The longer a pattern persists, the more familiar—and therefore safer—it feels. This is why the status quo often wins even when it is objectively harmful.

Disturb exists to gently disrupt that illusion of safety. You are not adding new fear; you are making the existing risk visible. You are helping the buyer understand why the pain they have learned to tolerate is no longer rational, sustainable, or defensible.

Buyer Psychology:
If the status quo feels safe, the buyer will not move. Disturb makes the real risk visible.

2. Purpose of Disturb

Disturb[17] is frequently misunderstood. It is not about provoking anxiety or forcing urgency. Fear-based tactics trigger resistance, defensiveness, and short-term decisions that ultimately collapse under internal scrutiny. Healthy Disturb has an entirely different intention.

Your role here is to name the risk the buyer is already living with, using evidence, patterns, and calmly delivered observations. You invite interpretation rather than panic. You respect the buyer's intelligence instead of trying to shock them. You illuminate the real cost of inaction without exaggeration.

When done correctly, Disturb does not feel like fear-mongering. It feels like clarity. Fear-mongering tries to provoke urgency. Disturb reveals consequence.

Petra's Insight:
Disturb works best when your tone is calm, your facts are grounded, and your intent is clearly to protect—not pressure—the buyer.

3. What Great Sounds Like

A great Disturb moment has a very specific signature. The founder speaks slowly, without urgency or drama. They name what is already happening inside the buyer's world, and they use simple cause-and-effect logic that immediately feels familiar. Buyers often interrupt with realizations of their own—"Yes, that's exactly what happens," or, "We've been feeling this for months but never articulated it."

A strong Disturb turns whispered frustrations into shared truth. It exposes the chain reaction created by seemingly small

---

17. Disturb reveals costs via chains, from Challenger "teach"—challenging assumptions lifts pipeline velocity 27%.

inefficiencies. It paints a picture the buyer instantly recognizes, not because it is new, but because it is finally put into words.

When done well, buyers frequently confess: "We *knew it was bad . . . but not this bad.*"

4. What Bad Sounds Like

Bad Disturb is easy to recognize. It feels like pressure. The founder dramatizes consequences, speaks in hypotheticals, or uses emotional language that makes the buyer feel manipulated. Blame, guilt, and shame enter the room. Instead of clarity, the conversation becomes adversarial.

Fear-mongering destroys trust because it signals that the founder cares more about advancing the deal than about helping the buyer think clearly.

Healthy Disturb does the opposite: it deepens trust by naming truths the buyer already lives with but has never fully examined.

5. Common Founder Mistakes in Disturb

Founders often fall into predictable traps: overstating risk, jumping into their pitch too soon, delivering Disturb with emotional charge rather than calm objectivity, or pointing to generic risks that have nothing to do with the buyer's actual world. Others fail to articulate upstream and downstream consequences, leaving the conversation trapped at surface-level fear rather than systemic clarity.

Perhaps the most common error is trying to *manufacture* urgency. Buyers do not respond to synthetic urgency—they retreat from it. They respond to clarity about what is already true.

The goal of Disturb is not pressure. It is **perspective**.

6. Business Reality: Where Disturb Lives

Disturb operates at the intersection of **hidden friction**, **underestimated risk**, and **lost opportunity**—the three forces that quietly erode performance inside every organization. These elements are rarely discussed openly because they are distributed across teams, embedded in legacy processes, and absorbed silently by individuals who have learned to compensate.

Decode reveals how work actually flows. Disturb reveals the cost of letting dysfunctional workarounds continue.

This is why Disturb feels so powerful to buyers: for the first time, someone connects the day-to-day frustrations with the strategic consequences leadership cares about.

Buyers often say: *"This finally explains why our team feels stretched all the time."*

7. Mini-Dialogue Example: Wayne and the Predictability Disturb

Wayne: Earlier you mentioned that priorities change mid-sprint and tickets get rewritten. How often does that happen in a typical month?

Engineering lead: Honestly? Almost every sprint. Something urgent comes in, or a spec wasn't clear enough.

Wayne: When a ticket is rewritten mid-sprint, what happens to the work that was originally planned?

Engineering lead: It gets pushed. Or people work late. Or we drop things quietly.

Wayne: And over a quarter, what does that do to predictability?

Engineering lead: It destroys it. Our roadmap becomes more of a wish list than a plan.

Wayne: If your roadmap is a wish list, how does that affect trust between Product, Engineering, and Leadership?

VP Product: It erodes it. People stop believing commitment dates.

Wayne noticed a pattern in engineering conversations: teams normalized chaos. He used Disturb to help them see the hidden cost.

When the engineering lead admitted that mid-sprint rewrites "destroyed predictability," Wayne gently connected the dots to trust erosion, missed commitments, and tension with leadership.

The insight wasn't dramatic. It was accurate. And because it was accurate, it was undeniable.

8. Core Disturb Questions

Use four to six of these questions per conversation to **surface risk calmly and objectively**. These prompts are designed to make hidden consequences visible without creating pressure, and to help buyers recognize the true cost of staying the same.

The goal is not to provoke fear—it is to reveal reality clearly enough that the buyer can no longer ignore it.

Each category surfaces a different dimension of hidden cost.

Breakpoints & Fragility Questions

These questions are designed to expose where the system fails under pressure:

- "When things get busy or stressful, what tends to break first?"
- "Which part of the process becomes unpredictable the fastest?"
- "In the last quarter, what failure pattern showed up more than once?"

Ownership & Exposure Questions

These questions reveal who absorbs the fallout and who quietly keeps problems from reaching leadership—a key indicator of organizational risk:

- "When something goes wrong, who steps in first to contain it?"
- "Who usually notices issues before customers or leadership does?"
- "Who carries the burden when this problem escalates?"

Escalation & Impact Questions

These questions highlight downstream consequences the buyer may have minimized:

- "How often do small issues turn into bigger ones?"
- "What does a single failure set in motion across other teams?"
- "What is the quarterly or annual cost of this friction—in time, error, or missed opportunities?"

Perspective Gap Questions

These questions uncover misalignment and differing interpretations across the organization:

- "Which teams see this problem differently—and why?"
- "Where do disagreements usually happen around this issue?"
- "Whose priorities conflict when this problem shows up?"

Trajectory & Risk Horizon Questions

These questions help the buyer see how the problem compounds over time:

- "If nothing changes in the next six months, what becomes harder or riskier?"

- "What does this issue threaten in the long term if it continues at the current rate?"
- "What's the worst-case scenario if this pattern persists?"
- "If this friction were removed, what would become easier or more predictable six months from now?"

All of these questions reveal truth without pressure, and risk without fear. They help buyers recognize the cost of the status quo—calmly, clearly, and on their own terms.

9. Stage Transition: How You Know Disturb Is Complete

Disturb is complete when the buyer begins shifting from description ("Here's what happens . . .") to evaluation ("We can't keep doing this . . .").

Move to **Reframe** only when:

- The buyer acknowledges unseen risk ("We didn't realize . . .")
- They verbalize consequences ("This is costing us more than we thought.")
- They shift from *describing* to *evaluating* ("If this continues . . .")
- They express emotional discomfort ("We can't keep doing this.")
- They begin asking future-oriented questions ("So what should we be doing instead?")

If these signals are missing, stay in Disturb longer.

10. Mastering Stage 3 – Disturb

Disturb requires calm precision, not force. The goal of the following exercises is to help founders practice revealing truth without triggering defensiveness—a skill that feels nuanced until you break it into deliberate practice. Each prompt below strengthens your ability to surface risk with clarity, protect the buyer's psychology, and create the kind of constructive tension that makes movement feel rational rather than risky.

Use these exercises to sharpen your Disturb narrative, deepen your diagnostic instincts, and refine your ability to illuminate consequences without slipping into pressure.

Exercises

1. **Identify five hidden risks your ICP (ideal customer profile) consistently overlooks.** Describe why each risk remains invisible inside their system and what normalizing it costs the organization over time.
2. **Map a friction chain: trigger → impact → consequence.** Take a real buyer situation and trace how a single breakdown cascades across teams, timelines, or customer experience.
3. **Write three Disturb questions that expose underappreciated risk.** Each question should reveal truth gently, without pressure or exaggeration.
4. **Draft a calm Disturb framing statement for a tense buyer.** Focus on tone and intent: your job is to help them think clearly, not to accelerate the deal.
5. **Revisit a moment where you held back a Disturb insight.** Rewrite how you would deliver it today using clarity, neutrality, and system-level reasoning.
6. **Set three tone guardrails for yourself.** Specify how you'll maintain objectivity, prevent dramatization, and keep the conversation grounded even when stakes are high.

What Disturb Looks Like in Practice

The goal of Disturb is not to alarm the buyer, but to surface risk that already exists—without exaggeration, pressure, or drama. The examples below are not scripts to memorize, but reference points to help you calibrate tone, intent, and structure.

Example: Disturb Questions That Expose Underappreciated Risk

These questions are designed to feel *thoughtful*, not confrontational. Notice that they point to consequences the buyer already lives with, rather than future hypotheticals.

- "When this process breaks down, who absorbs the cost first—before it ever reaches leadership?"
- "What work has your team normalized that would feel unacceptable if it were fully visible?"
- "If nothing changed here for the next twelve months, where would the pressure compound quietly rather than explode?"

Each question invites reflection without forcing urgency. The risk emerges through the buyer's own reasoning.

Example: A Calm Disturb Framing for a Tense Buyer

Disturb works best when you explicitly remove pressure before naming risk.

"I'm not raising this to accelerate anything today. I want to sanity-check something I'm noticing, because if I'm right, it may explain why this keeps resurfacing despite good effort."

This framing signals neutrality, shared exploration, and respect for the buyer's position—making it psychologically safe to engage with the uncomfortable truth.

Example: Revisiting a Held-Back Disturb Insight

Original moment (held back): The founder notices that delays are caused by leadership indecision—but avoids naming it.

Rewritten with Disturb clarity: "What I'm hearing is that the work doesn't stall because teams are misaligned—it stalls because approvals change once risk becomes visible. That puts teams in a position where speed and safety are constantly at odds."

This version replaces blame with system-level logic. It describes reality without assigning fault.

Example: Tone Guardrails for Disturb

Before entering any Disturb moment, founders should define guardrails that prevent escalation or dramatization. For example:

- **Neutrality:** Describe patterns, not people. Focus on behavior the system produces.
- **Precision:** Name specific consequences instead of broad warnings.
- **Restraint:** Stop once the risk is visible. Do not stack multiple disturbances at once.

These guardrails ensure Disturb remains a stabilizing force, not a trigger for defensiveness.

These exercises train the discipline behind effective Disturb: the ability to reveal what's already true—and impossible to ignore—without ever making the buyer feel cornered or judged.

ADVANCED DISTURB

(For enterprise, multi-team, technical, or political environments)

Hidden Risk Mapping Framework

In most organizations, the true cost of internal friction is profoundly underestimated. Decision-makers normalize inefficiencies because they live inside them every day: the manual rework no one has time to fix, the unpredictable workflows that disrupt planning cycles, the strained relationships between teams who blame each other instead of the system. As months pass, this friction becomes invisible—not because it disappears, but because teams unconsciously adapt around it.

Advanced Disturb surfaces this hidden cost architecture. It helps buyers see the *systemic exposure* created by inaction, not through pressure, but through structural clarity. These risks typically fall into three intertwined dimensions:

- **Operational Risk**—the erosion of predictability, consistency, and capacity. It shows up in chronic manual rework, unreliable handoffs, escalations, and near-miss failures that strain teams and distort planning.
- **Strategic Risk**—the long-term consequences of operational fragility: delays to critical initiatives, missed revenue windows, compromised roadmaps, and the gradual loss of competitive advantage.
- **Relationship Risk**—the human fallout: mistrust between departments, damaged customer confidence, reputation

concerns, and the political exposure that makes buyers hesitate.

When founders reveal these layers with calm precision, buyers finally see the *full cost of the status quo*. The shift is not emotional—it is cognitive. They understand, perhaps for the first time, the difference between "painful but manageable" and "quietly destructive."

Sector Examples: How Disturb Applies Across Industries

Disturb looks different in every domain, but the underlying mechanics are the same: systems absorb friction until they break, and leaders underestimate the cumulative cost until it is mapped clearly.

SaaS Product & Engineering

Unstable intake processes create unpredictable sprints; unpredictable sprints cause roadmap drift; roadmap drift erodes leadership trust. A founder who clearly connects this chain offers clarity no roadmap slide can match.

Cybersecurity

Slow incident response increases regulatory exposure; manual triage overwhelms teams, creating alert fatigue; alert fatigue produces blind spots that leadership never sees until it's too late. Disturb here is not fear—it is realism.

Logistics & Operations

Late throughput leads to downstream customer churn; manual correction generates overtime costs and burnout; overloaded supervisors make more errors, deepening the cycle. Mapping these domino effects turns scattered pain into a coherent narrative.

Manufacturing

Machine downtime stalls capacity; misaligned shift planning triggers safety risks; unpredictable output disrupts sales commitments and customer trust. Disturb reveals how "minor" delays cost millions in quiet opportunity loss.

In every sector, Disturb points to *systemic risk*. Not incompetence. Not personal failure. Simply the truth the organization has not yet articulated.

Founder Story: Jon and the Hidden Failure Pattern

Jon kept encountering the same surface-level complaint across multiple prospects: "Our automation keeps failing."

For months, he responded with product explanations—improved reliability, smarter triggers, better monitoring. Buyers nodded, agreed, and even praised the product . . . but nothing moved.

Once Jon adopted the Buyer Sense approach, he entered the conversation differently.

He no longer tried to defend automation. He tried to understand the *system behind the failure.*

Jon: When the automation fails, what happens in the next twenty-four hours?

Ops director: We revert to manual work. People stay late.

Jon: How often does that happen in a typical month?

Ops director: Six to eight times.

Jon: And who usually notices first—your team or your customers?

Ops director: If we're lucky, just us. If not, the customers.

Jon: When customers notice, how does it affect their trust?

Ops director: They start questioning our reliability. And once that happens . . . they start shopping around.

In less than ten minutes, Jon transformed the narrative. The real risk wasn't "automation downtime." It was **customer trust erosion**—a strategic vulnerability hiding beneath an operational nuisance.

By the end of the call, the Ops director said: "We've been treating this as an efficiency issue. It's actually a customer risk issue. We can't ignore this anymore."

Jon didn't pressure them. He didn't dramatize anything. He simply revealed what was already true—but hidden by habit.

That is the essence of Advanced Disturb.

STAGE 4 – REFRAME

1. Psychology of Reframe

Reframes work because the human brain is wired to seek coherence. When people encounter situations that feel ambiguous, contradictory, or overloaded with variables, their mental model begins to fracture. They cannot reliably judge risk, prioritize action, or interpret cause and effect. Cognitive scientists refer to this state as *disorganized complexity*: too many inputs, too many interpretations, and too much noise for the brain to process efficiently.

Modern buyers live in this state daily. Across functions and industries, they are navigating the following:

- Multiple variables that interact unpredictably
- Conflicting priorities between teams
- Unclear causal chains and feedback loops
- Internal politics that distort signal into noise

In this fog, buyers rely on familiar narratives—even if those narratives are incomplete or inaccurate—simply because the brain prefers a flawed model to no model at all.

A powerful Reframe interrupts that pattern not by adding new information, but by reorganizing existing information into a structure the mind can finally use. This is not persuasion. It is interpretation.

It gives the buyer a simpler, truer way to understand their

situation—a mental model[18] that reduces cognitive load and increases perceived control.

Buyer Psychology:
Confusion creates paralysis*. **Clarity creates momentum.***

2. Purpose of Reframe

The purpose of Stage 4 is to help the buyer *make meaning*. Decode uncovered how the system actually works. Disturb revealed the consequences of leaving it unchanged. Now, the buyer must integrate all that complexity into a coherent understanding.

Reframe accomplishes that by doing the following:

- Giving the buyer a new interpretive lens
- Connecting surface symptoms to hidden system dynamics
- Revealing the underlying logic beneath recurring issues
- Translating complexity into simplicity, without oversimplifying
- Shifting them from, "Something is wrong," to, "I finally understand what's wrong"

By the end of this stage, the buyer should feel an unmistakable sense of relief—the cognitive exhale that occurs when confusion collapses into understanding:

"Ah . . . now this makes sense."

---

18. Reframe shifts models, core to Adamson/Schmidt's Framemaking Sale (2025): shared frames slash 'no decision' from 62% to 24%

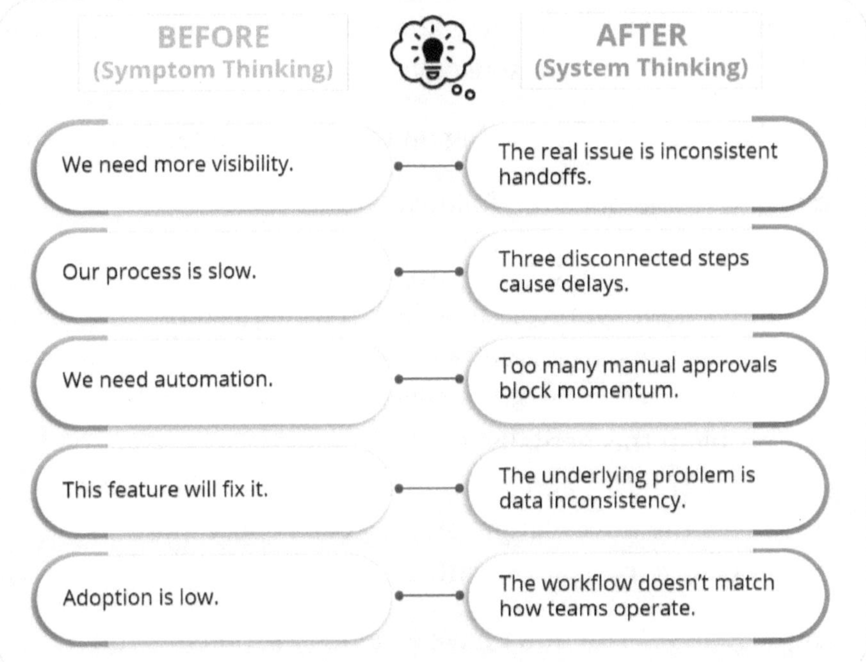

Figure 5: Pattern Reframes Matrix: Reframe from symptom thinking to system thinking.

Figure 5 illustrates the shift from symptom-based thinking to system-level understanding.

The left side shows common buyer statements that describe what feels wrong on the surface. The right side shows how those same issues are Reframed once the underlying system dynamics are understood. This matrix highlights how reframing does not change the problem itself—but changes how the problem is interpreted.

This clarity is what makes Stage 5 (ALIGN) possible.

3. What Great Sounds Like

A great Reframe does not challenge the buyer. It *relieves* them. It begins with the symptom they know, then gradually reveals the broader system they had sensed but could not articulate.

It sounds like someone turning on the lights in a familiar room.

A strong Reframe does the following:

- Starts with the buyer's own language
- Links their symptom to a deeper, recognizable root cause
- Shows the pattern across similar teams or companies
- Delivers a simple, stable way to understand what kind of problem this actually is
- Feels intuitive and obvious once stated—"Of course."
- Gives the buyer language they can repeat internally
- Replaces frustration with clarity

Example (SaaS): "You don't have a velocity problem—you have a predictability problem."

That sentence shifts the entire conversation from speed to structure.

4. What Bad Sounds Like

Bad Reframes introduce cleverness, ego, or contradiction into a moment where the buyer needs clarity and validation.

They fail when they feel as follows:

- Clever rather than clarifying
- Contrarian merely for effect
- Intellectually impressive but practically irrelevant
- Disconnected from the buyer's lived experience
- Rushed because the buyer hasn't had time to discover it
- Imposed instead of collaboratively surfaced

A Reframe collapses instantly if the buyer feels corrected, confused, or invalidated.

A Reframe must feel like **their insight**, not your performance.

5. Common Founder Mistakes in Reframe

Most failed Reframes trace back to timing and grounding. Founders often do the following:

- Jump to a Reframe too soon—before Decode and Disturb have built the foundation
- Offer a Reframe that does not match the actual system the buyer described
- Make the buyer feel subtly wrong or naive
- Rely on clever phrasing rather than real insight
- Skip showing the pattern across similar companies
- Fail to anchor the Reframe in the buyer's own words and examples

A Reframe only works when it emerges *from the buyer's reality*, not *from the founder's agenda*.

6. The Structure of a Signature Reframe

A signature Reframe follows a natural progression that mirrors how human cognition updates mental models:

1. **Begin with the familiar symptom**—the issue the buyer already acknowledges.
2. **Reveal the hidden root cause**—the upstream mechanism that explains the symptoms.
3. **Show the broader pattern**—how similar organizations experience the same dynamic.
4. **Provide a simple mental model**—a clear, repeatable way to understand the problem.

Founders who master this structure shift from "solution vendor" to "strategic advisor." That shift changes everything.

Petra's Insight:

*A **Reframe** is not invented—it is discovered by understanding the system better than the buyer.*

7. Mini-Dialogue Example: Matt and the Predictability Reframe

Matt met a VP of Product who insisted the core issue was engineering velocity.

VP Product: We just need Engineering to move faster.

Rather than contradicting directly, Matt led the VP to his own insight:

Matt: If Engineering delivered faster, would your roadmap still slip when priorities change mid-sprint?

The VP paused. His mental model cracked open.

Matt: From what I'm seeing in teams like yours, the issue usually isn't speed—it's predictability.

The VP exhaled. His frustration had found a name.

VP Product: That . . . actually makes sense. Our issues start before Engineering even touches the work.

That single sentence unlocked cross-team alignment and shifted the agenda entirely.

Matt didn't win by selling harder.
He won by reframing more precisely.

8. Core Reframe Questions

Use a small handful of questions—two to four is more than enough—to guide the buyer gently toward the insight rather than delivering it outright. The purpose here is not interrogation, but discovery. Your questions should invite reflection and help the buyer see the deeper pattern emerging beneath the symptoms.

Examples of questions that naturally open the path to a Reframe include the following:

- "How do you think this issue begins upstream, before it becomes visible?"
- "When this happens across teams, what pattern do you tend to see repeat?"
- "What seems to be the common thread behind these different symptoms?"
- "If this problem disappeared tomorrow, what do you think would break next?"
- "Where does the real instability seem to originate?"
- "Does this resemble what you're observing in other parts of the organization?"

These questions do not *deliver* the Reframe. They simply create the cognitive space in which the buyer can arrive at it themselves.

9. Stage Transition: How You Know Reframe Is Complete

You'll know the Reframe has landed when the buyer begins to treat the new mental model as their own. They will often verbalize it spontaneously, sometimes with relief, sometimes with quiet recognition. You may hear sentences like, "This actually explains everything," or see subtle signals like a shift in posture, a moment of silence, or a thoughtful pause as their cognitive load decreases.

A complete Reframe becomes clear when the buyer starts exploring implications—asking questions that begin with phrases like, "If that's true, then . . ."—or explaining the insight back to you in their own words. You may also notice a shift from tactical thinking ("We just need X to work faster") to strategic interpretation ("The real instability is upstream, not in our execution").

If the buyer still seems uncertain, continues listing symptoms, or remains stuck in their original framing of the problem, then the Reframe has not fully integrated yet. Stay in the stage longer, slow the conversation down, and let the clarity emerge naturally.

10. Mastering Stage 4 – Reframe

Reframe is the discipline of turning complexity into coherence. The goal of this exercise is to help founders practice translating what buyers already know—but cannot yet organize—into a clear, repeatable mental model that reduces confusion and enables alignment.

These prompts strengthen your ability to surface insight without contradiction, deliver clarity without ego, and help buyers make sense of their situation in a way that holds once the conversation ends.

- **Write down three recurring symptoms your ICP mentions**—the language buyers use before they have clarity.
- **Identify the hidden root cause beneath each symptom**, based on patterns you consistently see across similar companies.
- **Draft one Signature Reframe for each symptom**, using the structure: symptom → hidden pattern → simple mental model.
- **Create a concise mental model** that captures the essence of the Reframe in a way a buyer can easily repeat internally.
- **Write a dialogue line in which the buyer discovers the insight themselves**, reflecting how the Reframe would naturally emerge in conversation.

- **Test each Reframe with a colleague or another founder**, ensuring it feels intuitive, relieving, and grounded in the buyer's lived experience.

What Reframe Looks Like in Practice

The goal of Reframe is not to correct the buyer, but to **organize their reality**. Strong Reframes feel obvious once stated. They replace fragmented explanations with a single, stable way to interpret what's happening.

The examples below are not scripts to memorize, but reference points to help you calibrate structure, tone, and depth.

Example 1: SaaS Product & Engineering

Buyer symptom (what they say): "Engineering just isn't moving fast enough."

Hidden pattern (what's actually happening): Unstable intake and shifting priorities destroy predictability, not effort or skill.

Signature Reframe: "You don't have a velocity problem—you have a predictability problem."

Simple mental model: Unstable inputs → broken commitments → perceived slowness

Buyer discovery moment (dialogue):

Founder: "If Engineering moved faster, would the roadmap still slip when priorities change mid-sprint?"

Buyer: (pause) "Yes . . . that's when everything breaks."

Founder: "Then speed isn't the constraint—predictability is."

This Reframe removes blame, explains recurring frustration, and gives the buyer language leadership can align around.

Example 2: Cybersecurity / IT Operations

Buyer symptom (what they say): "We're drowning in alerts."

Hidden pattern (what's actually happening): Low signal reliability forces analysts into constant triage and erodes trust in the system.

Signature Reframe: "You don't have an alert volume issue—you have a signal reliability issue."

Simple mental model: Unreliable signals → manual judgment → alert fatigue → missed risk

Buyer discovery moment (dialogue):

Founder: "If alerts were cut in half tomorrow, would response accuracy improve?"

Buyer: "Honestly? No. We still wouldn't trust what we're seeing."

Founder: "Right—so the issue isn't volume. It's signal reliability."

The Reframe shifts the conversation from tooling to trust, making the real risk discussable without fear.

Example 3: Operations/Supply Chain

Buyer symptom (what they say): "We need better visibility."

Hidden pattern (what's actually happening): Inconsistent handoffs and ownership gaps create blind spots, not lack of data.

Signature Reframe: "You don't have a visibility problem—you have an ownership consistency problem."

Simple mental model: Unclear ownership → broken handoffs → reactive visibility requests

Buyer discovery moment (dialogue):

Founder: "When something goes wrong, do you usually lack data—or lack clarity on who owns the next step?"

Buyer: (exhales) "Ownership. Every time."

Founder: "That's the system breaking—not visibility."

This Reframe replaces tool-seeking behavior with structural understanding.

Reframe Calibration Note

Across all examples, notice what does *not* happen:

- No contradiction
- No clever phrasing for its own sake
- No urgency or pressure

A strong Reframe feels relieving because it gives the buyer **a cleaner way to think**, not a new thing to defend.

These exercises train the discipline behind effective Reframe: the ability to convert scattered symptoms into a shared mental model that buyers can carry into alignment, prioritization, and action.

ADVANCED REFRAME

*(For enterprise, multi-team, technical,
or political environments)*

Why Advanced Reframes Matter in Complex Deals

In simple sales cycles, a Reframe is a helpful insight. In complex sales cycles, a Reframe is the **only mechanism** that creates shared understanding across a fragmented organization.

Enterprise buyers rarely suffer from a lack of expertise. They suffer from **interpretive fragmentation**—each team sees a different slice of the truth, filtered through their own incentives, pressures, and political constraints.

In that environment, the buyer's "mental model" isn't just incomplete—it is **splintered across departments**. No single stakeholder has the whole picture, and no one has the authority or psychological safety to name what's actually happening.

A strong Reframe does three things at once:

1. **It unifies multiple perspectives into one coherent narrative.**
2. **It offers a politically safe explanation that no one needs to defend against.**
3. **It becomes the internal language teams use to make decisions.**

This is why advanced Reframes must be as follows:

- Neutral enough that no team feels blamed

- Factual enough that no one can dispute them
- Pattern-based enough to feel inevitable
- Discovered collaboratively rather than imposed
- Framed gently enough to avoid triggering resistance

A Reframe fails when it threatens someone's territory. A Reframe succeeds when it gives everyone a clearer way to think.

It answers the silent, organization-wide question:

"What is actually going on here—and how should we make sense of it?"

A weak Reframe adds noise. A strong Reframe eliminates noise and gives the company a single, shared mental model.

Buyer Psychology (Advanced):
In complex sales, buyers don't follow the smartest idea. They follow the explanation everyone can live with.

Sector Reframes: High-Impact Examples

Across industries, the strongest Reframes replace **local symptoms** with **systemic explanations**—the shift buyers were unconsciously searching for.

SaaS/Product Teams

Symptom: "Engineering is too slow."

Advanced Reframe: "You don't have a velocity problem—you have a predictability problem."

Cybersecurity

Symptom: "We're drowning in alerts."

Advanced Reframe: "You don't have an alert volume issue—you have a signal reliability issue."

Logistics/Supply Chain

Symptom: "We need more productivity."

Advanced Reframe: "You don't have a productivity issue—you have a throughput consistency issue."

Manufacturing

Symptom: "Downtime is killing us."

Advanced Reframe: "You don't have a downtime issue—you have a capacity reliability problem."

Each Reframe shifts the conversation from **symptom to system**, which is what creates alignment, urgency, and executive ownership.

The Reframe Builder Tool

Use this structure to craft Reframes that both clarify the system and survive internal politics.

1. Start with their symptom.

"You mentioned ___________________happens often."

2. Reveal the hidden upstream cause.

"From what I'm seeing, this typically stems from __________."

3. Show the cross-company pattern.

"Teams like yours often experience X because of Y."

4. Deliver the unifying Reframe.

"So the real issue isn't A—it's B."

Example

"You don't have a productivity issue—you have a throughput consistency issue."

This is what converts complexity into coherence.

Advanced Reframe Patterns

These patterns reflect the most common systemic misunderstandings across industries. They are "templates" your clients will universally recognize.

Pattern 1: Resource → Flow

"This isn't a resource issue—it's a flow stability issue."

Pattern 2: Speed → Predictability

"This isn't about going faster—it's about making outcomes reliable."

Pattern 3: Volume → Quality

"This isn't a volume problem—this is a signal quality problem."

Pattern 4: Symptom → System Architecture

"This isn't a symptom—it's a systemic architecture issue."

These patterns not only Reframe—they elevate. They help the buyer shift from operational firefighting to strategic understanding.

STAGE 5 – ALIGN

Create Shared Interpretation • Build Internal Agreement • Enable Collective Movement

1. Psychology of Align

After Reframe, the buyer finally sees their world with new clarity. They understand the true problem, its upstream drivers, and the systemic consequences. But insight alone does not produce movement. **Inside any organization, movement requires agreement.**

This is where most deals begin to fracture.

Human beings do not act on individual understanding when they work inside systems. They act on **shared understanding**—and only when that understanding feels politically safe, functionally coherent, and strategically viable.

Research across organizational psychology (Weick), decision science (Simon), and power dynamics (Pfeffer) consistently shows:[19]

- People interpret the same situation differently depending on their incentives, identity, and exposure.
- Conflicting interpretations create political tension, even when everyone "agrees" that something is wrong.

---

19. Karl E. Weick, *Sensemaking in Organizations* (Thousand Oaks, CA: Sage Publications, 1995); Herbert A. Simon, *Administrative Behavior: A Study of Decision-Making Processes in Administrative Organizations*, 4th ed. (New York: Free Press, 1997 [1947]); Jeffrey Pfeffer, *Power in Organizations* (Marshfield, MA: Pitman, 1981).

- Organizations move only when multiple stakeholders adopt the same mental model.

Align exists to unify these mental models.

It transforms an individual insight into collective readiness. Because buyers don't move simply because *you* make sense. They move when **their organization makes sense to itself**.

Buyer Psychology:
People don't act when they agree with you.
They act when they agree with each other.

2. Purpose of Align

The purpose of Align is to guide the buyer from *personal recognition* to *organizational coherence*. In this stage, your role shifts from interpreter to facilitator—someone who helps the buyer translate the Reframe into a shared narrative their peers can adopt.

Align ensures that:

- The Reframe becomes a **collective lens**, not a personal insight.
- Different teams interpret the problem through the **same story**, not competing stories.
- Political tensions surface early, instead of sabotaging the deal later.
- Criteria for evaluating solutions are **co-created**, not inherited or dictated.
- Leadership receives a narrative that fits their timing, priorities, and risk appetite.

By the end of Align, the buyer should feel:

"Everyone sees this the same way—we can move."

Without this stage, alignment remains shallow, fragile, and personal. And personal alignment collapses under organizational friction.

3. What Great Sounds Like

A great alignment conversation feels like **strategic synthesis**, not persuasion. The founder listens deeply, integrates perspectives, and holds space for unresolved tensions without rushing to solutioning.

Great Align moments sound like:

- "It sounds like each of you sees a different piece of the same system—let's map them together."
- "Here's the thread I'm hearing across all your descriptions . . ."
- "Can I reflect something back? It seems you all agree on X, even if you frame it differently."

The tone is steady, respectful, and grounded. Stakeholders feel seen—not corrected. Differences become data—not conflict.

When Align is working, stakeholders begin to say:

"Yes—this is exactly how we should talk about this internally."

At that moment, you're no longer selling—you're shaping the organization's internal language.

4. What Bad Sounds Like

Misalignment rarely announces itself. It hides inside polite nods, enthusiastic champions, and reassuring phrases like, *"I'll bring this back to the team."* On the surface, everything looks cooperative. Beneath the surface, contradictory interpretations remain unresolved and begin to drift apart.

Bad Align moments occur when founders:

- Mistake early enthusiasm for organizational consensus

- Win over one individual but ignore cross-functional implications
- Allow political tension to simmer unaddressed
- Move forward before the narrative is stable across teams
- Outsource internal alignment to the buyer without providing support

This is how deals die—not dramatically, but quietly. Weeks later, the founder hears the familiar sentence: *"We've decided not to move forward right now."*

Bad alignment creates stalled momentum, internal friction, leadership skepticism, and the silent death of "no decision," a decision that materializes only after you're no longer in the room.

5. Common Founder Mistakes in Align

Most alignment failures stem from misunderstanding organizational dynamics. Founders often:

- Treat a champion's excitement as system-level agreement
- Overlook how different teams interpret the same problem
- Avoid the political reality that each function protects its own priorities
- Jump prematurely into solutioning
- Fail to co-create buying criteria
- Assume the buyer can "handle" internal alignment alone

These mistakes turn alignment into a bottleneck instead of a bridge. And the result is always the same:

Deals die in meetings you weren't invited to.

6. Business Reality: Where Align Lives

The Alignment Layers

Every complex B2B decision moves through three psychological and organizational layers. A deal only becomes real when all three align. Most founders stop at personal agreement, unaware that deeper layers must also shift before an organization can take action.

Alignment must happen across **three layers**, each with its own psychology:

1. Personal Alignment

The individual stakeholder accepts the Reframe and feels the problem deserves attention.

2. Functional Alignment

Teams such as Engineering, Product, Operations, Finance, IT, and Security reach a shared interpretation—even if their incentives differ.

3. Strategic Alignment

Leadership, planning cycles, budget windows, and organizational priorities line up with the proposed direction.

Most deals collapse because founders mistake personal alignment for system alignment. But insight must cascade through all three layers before action is possible.

Align is the stage where that cascade begins.

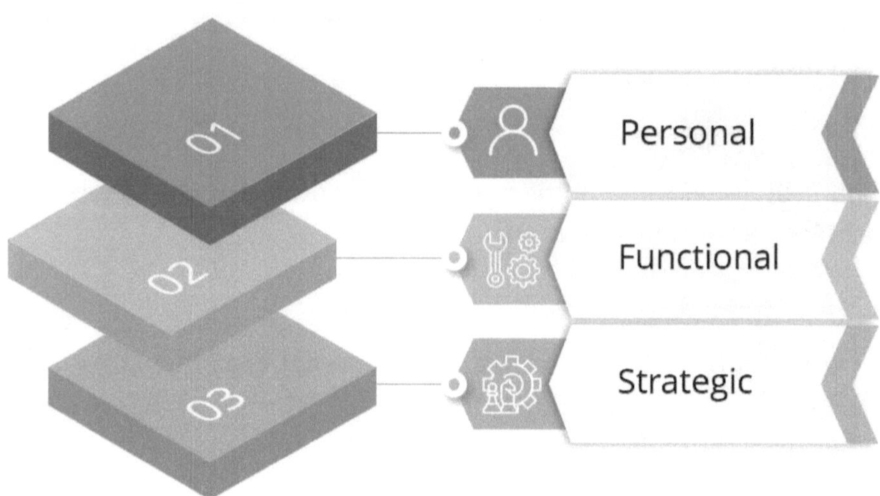

Figure 6: The Alignment Layers

This figure 6 shows the three layers that must align for a decision to move forward: individual understanding, cross-functional agreement, and strategic fit with leadership priorities and timing. Deals stall when founders confuse personal agreement with organizational readiness. True alignment requires all three layers to move together.

7. Mini-Dialogue Example: When Alignment Breaks Down

David once worked with a VP of Product who fully embraced the Reframe. The VP could articulate the predictability issue clearly, understood the systemic root cause, and appeared ready to move forward. But alignment at the individual level can be profoundly misleading.

When David asked whether Engineering should join the next conversation, the VP waved the suggestion away: *"Let's finalize this first—I'll handle Engineering."*

David agreed, assuming the VP's confidence reflected broader buy-in. It didn't.

A week passed with no movement. When David finally spoke to the Engineering lead, the illusion shattered. The lead dismissed the Reframed problem entirely: *"Predictability? No—our real issue is capacity."*

In that moment, David saw the deeper truth: **the deal had never been aligned—only one person was**. The conversation would need to return almost to the beginning, because alignment with a single stakeholder does not survive contact with organizational reality.

Petra's Insight:
If alignment skips even one important stakeholder, the deal resets to zero.

8. Core Align Questions

Alignment requires widening the buyer's field of vision beyond their own function. To do that, founders ask questions that gently reveal the broader system without triggering defensiveness. These questions don't interrogate—they illuminate. They help the buyer see the political, functional, and strategic terrain surrounding the problem.

A founder might begin by exploring who else absorbs the downstream impact of the issue, prompting the buyer to recognize that friction rarely ends within a single department. They may then explore how other teams interpret the same situation—not to expose disagreement, but to surface the parallel narratives that exist inside every organization.

Another moment of clarity comes when the founder asks who must feel comfortable before anything can move forward. This question shifts the frame from *individual alignment* to *organizational readiness*, and helps the buyer map the internal decision chain with more honesty.

Finally, a founder may ask what leadership will need to see, understand, or believe in order to support a new direction. This elevates the conversation from functional alignment to strategic alignment—the point where decisions are actually made.

Used well, these questions guide the buyer from personal insight to shared interpretation. They help transform a good conversation into an aligned organization.

To anchor the process, here are the four Core Align Questions:

1. **"Who else experiences the impact of this problem?"**
2. **"How do other teams interpret this situation today?"**
3. **"Who needs to feel comfortable before this moves forward?"**
4. **"What will leadership need to see or understand to support this direction?"**

These questions shift the buyer from an individual understanding of the problem to an organizational alignment around what truly needs to change.

9. Stage Transition: How You Know Align Is Complete

You only move into prioritize when alignment is no longer a personal feeling but an organizational fact. At this point, the Reframe has travelled beyond your primary contact, different teams are using the same language, and the path forward has been discussed explicitly rather than assumed.

Look for signals such as:

- The buyer can confidently articulate the Reframe in their own words.
- Cross-functional teams echo the same (shared) interpretation of the problem.
- Political contradictions or tensions have been surfaced and addressed.

- Leadership-level conversations are happening, with clear sponsorship or curiosity.
- Buying criteria have been co-created, and there is agreement on how decisions will be made.
- The buyer says some version of: **"This is the direction we all agree on."**

If these signals are weak, inconsistent, or missing, you are not finished with Align. Stay in this stage and keep working on shared interpretation before you move the conversation toward timing and prioritization.

10. Mastering Stage 5—Align

Alignment is where individual conviction either becomes shared organizational truth—or quietly fragments once the conversation leaves the room.

Founders often believe alignment has happened because one buyer "gets it." In reality, alignment only exists when multiple teams— each with different incentives, risks, and priorities—interpret the problem in the same way. Until that happens, progress remains fragile, no matter how positive the conversations feel.

The purpose of this section is to help you turn alignment from an assumption into a deliberate practice.

The exercises below are designed to help you surface hidden misalignment early, unify competing interpretations, and build a shared narrative that can survive internal meetings you will never attend.

Exercises

1. **List three real deals that stalled or went to "no decision" because of hidden misalignment.** These are deals that felt positive, logical, and promising—but never moved forward.
2. **For each deal, map how every key team interpreted**

the problem differently. Include Product, Operations, Finance, IT, Security, Leadership—any group that would be affected or asked to approve.

3. **Rewrite those conflicting interpretations into a single, shared framing.** This framing should feel accurate, neutral, and safe for all teams to support—even if it does not fully match any one group's original view.

4. **Draft three alignment-building questions you will deliberately use in future calls.** These questions should expand the conversation beyond one stakeholder and surface organizational reality.

5. **Take one active deal and map the full internal decision chain using the Alignment Builder Tool.**

6. **Co-create a simple set of buying criteria with a champion.** These criteria should reflect the shared framing and help the buyer guide internal evaluation consistently.

What Alignment Looks Like in Practice

Alignment work does not feel like selling. It feels like facilitation, translation, and synthesis. The examples below are not scripts to memorize—they are reference points to help you recognize alignment dynamics in real conversations.

Scenario 1: The Enthusiastic Champion, Fragmented Organization

Signal: Your main contact is excited and confident, but phrases like, "I'll take this to the team," or, "I'll handle the rest," keep appearing.

Hidden reality: Personal alignment exists. Functional and strategic alignment do not.

Alignment move: "Before you take this forward internally, can we map how Engineering, Finance, and Leadership currently describe this issue? I want to make sure the story holds once it leaves this room."

Desired buyer thought: "This needs alignment before advocacy."

Scenario 2: Teams Agree There's a Problem—but Not What the Problem Is

Signal: Everyone agrees something isn't working, but each function names a different cause.

- Product: "Engineering is too slow."
- Engineering: "Requirements keep changing."
- Finance: "Costs are unpredictable."
- Leadership: "We miss commitments."

Alignment move: "It sounds like each team is describing a symptom of the same system. Can we map the sequence together—from intake to delivery—so we're all reacting to the same underlying issue?"

Shared framing example: "This isn't a speed or capacity issue. It's a predictability issue created by unstable intake and shifting approvals."

Desired buyer thought: "We're not misaligned—we're misinterpreting the same problem."

Scenario 3: The Buyer Wants to Move Forward—but Leadership Feels Hesitant

Signal: The buyer says, "Leadership is cautious," or "They'll need to be convinced."

Hidden reality: Strategic alignment has not formed. Risk feels unmanaged.

Alignment move: "What do you think leadership would need to understand for this to feel like a responsible decision rather than a risky one?"

Desired buyer thought: "This needs framing, not persuasion."

The Alignment Builder Tool

The Alignment Builder Tool is not a framework or template. It is a live mapping approach that helps you assess whether a deal can survive internal scrutiny.

It is designed to be used inside real conversations, not as a document the buyer ever sees.

Its purpose is to answer one critical question:

Do the people who matter interpret this problem the same way?

How the Alignment Builder Tool Works

Use this map conversationally, not formally:

1. **Who is affected by this problem?** (Not who is on the call—who absorbs the impact.)
2. **How does each group currently describe the issue?** (Surface differences without judgment.)
3. **Where do those interpretations conflict?** (This is where deals usually stall.)
4. **What shared framing could all teams agree is true?** (System-level, neutral, non-blaming.)
5. **Who must feel comfortable before anything can move forward?** (This reveals the real decision chain.)

If you cannot answer these five questions clearly, alignment does not yet exist—regardless of buyer enthusiasm.

Alignment Builder in Action

Founder: Who else feels the impact when this breaks?

Buyer: Engineering, Operations, and Finance.

Founder: And how does each team describe the issue today?

Buyer: Engineering says intake is chaotic. Ops says delivery is unpredictable. Finance worries about cost variance.

Founder: So different symptoms—but one system. What do they all agree on?

Buyer: (long pause) That commitments keep changing.

Founder: Then maybe the shared issue isn't speed or cost—it's commitment stability.

Co-Creating Buying Criteria

Once alignment exists, buying criteria should emerge naturally from the shared framing.

Use questions like:

- "Given this issue, what must any solution do to truly fix it?"
- "What risks would leadership push back on unless addressed upfront?"
- "What would make Engineering and Finance both feel safe supporting this?"

These criteria become the internal evaluation lens the buyer can reuse consistently.

ADVANCED ALIGN

(For enterprise, multi-team, technical, or political environments)

Why Advanced Alignment Determines Deal Survival

In complex buying environments, alignment is less about agreement and more about narrative convergence. Every function carries its own mental model of the problem, shaped by incentives, workload, risk sensitivity, and political exposure. Those models rarely match—and they never match by accident.

Advanced Align works because it replaces competing narratives with a shared interpretation that feels politically safe, functionally accurate, and strategically relevant. Once that shared interpretation exists, movement becomes possible. Without it, even the strongest insight dies inside a meeting you never attend.

Advanced reality: Organizations do not buy the best solution. They buy the solution that *everyone can live with.*

Buyer Psychology
Alignment begins with shared interpretation—long before shared decisions.

Dialogue Scene: Building Shared Interpretation

Founder (Barbara): If we're going to solve predictability, who else needs to be part of this?

VP Product: Engineering and Ops, definitely.

Barbara: How do they interpret the problem today?

VP Product: (*long pause*) Engineering thinks it's a capacity issue. Ops thinks it's a process issue. Leadership thinks it's an accountability issue.

Barbara: So each group sees a different problem. Unless we bring them into the same framing, the teams will fight each other—not the problem.

VP Product: . . . Yes. That is exactly what keeps happening.

Barbara: Then let's align interpretation first. The solution comes second.

This is alignment at the strategic level—shrinking political noise by giving every team the same language and lens.

Founder Story: How Jodie Created Executive Alignment

Jodie met with a COO who loved her solution. But the CFO and plant manager held competing narratives:

CFO: Our biggest issue is overtime cost.

Plant manager: No—the issue is process ownership.

COO: None of that matters if throughput keeps skipping steps.

Most founders would pick a side. Jodie didn't.

Jodie: It sounds like you're each describing different symptoms of the same system. Can we map the sequence together?

In ten minutes, they uncovered the hidden chain:

- Skipped steps →
- led to delays →
- which triggered overtime →
- all caused by unclear process ownership →
- amplified by misaligned priorities.

Jodie didn't align them to *her solution*. She aligned them to *each other*.

The deal closed in twenty-one days.

Connecting the Reframe to the Correct Solution Type

Once a buyer accepts the Reframe, their next internal question is not:

"Which vendor?" but, **"Which *type* of solution solves this root cause?"**

This is the founder's opportunity to define the strategic playing field.

Examples of Solution Type Fit:

- **Predictability issue** → stability and intake-control tools, not speed accelerators.
- **Signal reliability issue** → noise-filtering and correlation systems, not automation engines.
- **Throughput inconsistency** → coordination and synchronization layers, not additional dashboards.

The goal is not to sell your product—it is to shape the *solution category* so your product becomes the natural fit.

Petra's Insight:
If you define the solution type correctly, you win before the demo even begins.

Co-Creating Buying Criteria (Without Selling)

Founders often try to "match" criteria the buyer already has. Advanced founders *co-create* the criteria with them.

This does three things simultaneously:

1. Aligns stakeholders around the Reframe

2. Reduces political friction
3. Makes the buyer committed to the criteria they helped define—criteria competitors usually **cannot** meet.

Examples:

- "What must any solution do to fix predictability long-term?"
- "Which risks must be eliminated first?"
- "What needs to feel true for Engineering and Ops to be comfortable?"
- "What would leadership push back on unless we address it upfront?"

You are guiding judgment, not selling features.

When criteria are co-authored, they become non-negotiable—and they naturally favor you.

The Alignment Builder Tool

The Alignment Builder Tool helps you translate insight into organizational agreement by making conflicting interpretations visible, reconcilable, and safe to align around before any decision is pushed forward.

See example below and then use the proposed sequence to guide cross-functional alignment inside the buyer's organization:

1. **"How does each team currently describe the problem?"** (Reveal narrative fragmentation.)
2. **"Where do interpretations differ?"** (Surface political and functional tension.)
3. **"What truth do all teams agree on?"** (Anchor the Reframe into shared reality.)
4. **"What buying criteria make sense given that truth?"** (Co-create the decision framework.)
5. **"Who must feel comfortable before we proceed?"** (Map the real decision chain.)

6. **"What timing constraints matter to leadership?"**
   (Align solution direction with organizational cycles.)

This is how Alignment becomes a **system**, not a hope.

Example: Alignment Builder Tool in Practice

Below is an example of how this sequence might unfold in a real enterprise deal, where enthusiasm exists but alignment is fragile.

Context:

A SaaS founder is selling into a mid-sized enterprise. The VP of Operations is the champion. Engineering, Finance, and Leadership will all influence the decision.

1. **How does each team currently describe the problem?**
   - Operations: "Delivery timelines are unpredictable."
   - Engineering: "Requirements change too often."
   - Finance: "Costs keep fluctuating quarter to quarter."
   - Leadership: "We miss commitments and lose credibility."

2. **Where do interpretations differ?** Each team sees a different symptom and assumes a different root cause—speed, discipline, or cost control—creating silent disagreement about what actually needs to change.

3. **What truth do all teams agree on?** Commitments are unstable. What gets promised at the start rarely holds through execution.

4. **What buying criteria make sense given that truth?** Any solution must stabilize intake, reduce late-stage changes, and improve predictability across teams—not just increase speed or automate tasks.

5. **Who must feel comfortable before we proceed?** Engineering leadership and Finance must believe this will reduce rework and cost volatility. Executive leadership must see how it improves forecast reliability.

6. **What timing constraints matter to leadership?** Budget planning closes in eight weeks. Any proposal must support the next planning cycle, not disrupt it.

At the end of this exercise, the founder and buyer are no longer "aligned" in sentiment—they are aligned in interpretation, criteria, and readiness.

What to Do with This Information

Use the output of the Alignment Builder Tool to **pressure-test whether a deal is actually ready to move forward**. If interpretations, criteria, or decision ownership remain unclear, pause progression and return to alignment—because momentum built on misalignment will collapse later, out of sight.

STAGE 6 – PRIORITIZE

1. Psychology of Prioritize

By the time a buyer reaches this stage, they understand the root cause of their problem, the system that produces it, and the consequences of letting it persist. Their mental model is clearer, and their confidence is higher. But *clarity is not commitment*—not yet.

Across decades of behavioral economics, researchers have shown that human beings consistently postpone action when the future feels abstract or emotionally distant. This tendency, known as **temporal discounting**[20] describes how people systematically undervalue future consequences while overvaluing the immediate comfort of "later." Even when the logic for action is sound, the brain instinctively prefers the psychological safety of delay.

In buying environments, temporal discounting becomes amplified by organizational realities. It shows up when the following is true:

- The **cost of waiting remains invisible**, buried inside day-to-day friction
- Consequences sit **too far downstream** to trigger urgency

---

20. Ainslie, George. *Psychological Bulletin*, 1975 – introduced hyperbolic discounting; people overvalue the comfort of "later."; Laibson, David. QJE, 1997 – formalized temporal discounting; future consequences feel less important.

- **Leadership timing** cycles (budget, planning, risk review) are not yet connected to the decision
- Operational friction has been **normalized** to the point where teams no longer feel its weight
- "Later" feels **emotionally safer** than "now," especially in politically exposed roles

Research by Kahneman and Tversky also shows that people overweight immediate loss and underweight delayed risk.[21] In corporate buying, this means the following:

Putting a decision off feels like avoiding risk; acting now feels like inviting it.

This is why prioritization cannot rely on pressure. Pressure activates loss aversion and defensiveness. The real work of Prioritize is to **help the buyer perceive the true timeline they are already operating within**—the operational, strategic, and political clocks that continue ticking whether they act or not.

When buyers finally see these timelines clearly, the decision to move forward stops feeling risky and begins to feel **rational, timely, and safe.**

Buyer Psychology:
People rarely delay decisions because they disagree with a solution. They delay because they cannot yet feel the timing consequences of inaction.

2. Purpose of Prioritize

The purpose of this stage is to convert insight into momentum. Prioritize makes the invisible visible: what grows more costly with delay—and what becomes unavailable if action waits too long.

---

21. Kahneman & Tversky. *Econometrica*, 1979 – loss aversion causes people to overweigh short-term risk and underweigh long-term risk.

In this stage, you help the buyer do the following:

- Understand what deteriorates, escalates, or becomes more expensive over time
- Recognize what opportunities are only available in the current window
- Connect operational consequences to leadership cycles and decision rhythms
- Anchor urgency in *their* world, not in your pipeline
- Recognize that delaying is not neutral—it is a choice with consequences

By the end of Prioritize, the buyer should feel an unmistakable shift from,
"Maybe later," to, "It will cost us more to wait than to act now."

3. What Great Sounds Like

A great prioritization moment does not sound dramatic or forceful. It sounds observational, grounded, and gentle—almost like you're holding up a mirror to the truth they already suspect.

A skilled founder:

- Reveals natural consequences without exaggeration
- Ties timing to the buyer's own metrics and internal cycles
- Shows how friction compounds over weeks, quarters, and planning cycles
- Helps the buyer connect delay → impact → risk
- Illuminates windows of opportunity that close or shift over time
- Makes timing feel practical, not emotional

When prioritization is done well, buyers often say something like:

"We can't afford to wait on this."

Not because you pushed them—but because you helped them see.

4. What Bad Sounds Like

Bad prioritization is urgency theater. It sounds like pressure, and buyers instinctively retreat from it.

It shows up when a founder does the following:

- Manufactures artificial urgency
- Uses fear instead of insight
- Exaggerates consequences
- Pushes toward closing instead of clarifying timing
- Frames urgency in terms of *their* timeline, not the buyer's
- Treats the buyer as if they are being slow, rather than thoughtful

Pressure triggers resistance. Clarity triggers movement.

5. Common Founder Mistakes in Prioritize

Many founders hesitate to have timing conversations at all—and lose momentum as a result. Others jump straight to pricing, assuming alignment automatically converts into action.

The most common mistakes include:

- Avoiding timing because it feels "salesy"
- Assuming alignment = commitment
- Introducing urgency too early, before clarity is established
- Ignoring leadership cycles and governance rhythms
- Failing to calculate or articulate the real cost of waiting
- Pushing deadlines instead of revealing natural consequences

The result is predictable: Deals die the slow, quiet death of *later*.

Prioritize prevents that by grounding urgency in truth, not pressure.

6. Business Reality: Where Prioritization Lives

Prioritization lives at the intersection of three realities:

1. The Consequence of Waiting

What worsens, breaks, or becomes more expensive or more politically exposed if nothing changes?

2. The Opportunity Window

What becomes possible sooner—strategically, financially, operationally—if the issue is addressed now?

3. Leadership Timing

Every organization runs on cycles: planning, budgeting, forecasting, risk review, compliance windows, and board meetings. Most buyers underestimate how these rhythms shape the "real" timeline.

Your role is not to impose urgency. Your role is to **reveal the timeline they are already operating within.**

7. Mini-Dialogue Example: The Cost of Waiting

Founder (Jon): If nothing changes this quarter, what happens to throughput consistency?

Ops director: It stays unstable.

Jon: And who absorbs that instability first?

Ops director: My team. And eventually our customers.

Jon: And if customers begin to feel it?

Ops director (*sighs*): They churn. We're already starting to see signs.

Jon: So the real decision isn't "solve this now or later." It's "solve it—or accept churn risk."

Ops director: Yeah . . . we can't afford to wait.

Buyer Psychology:
Urgency emerges naturally when buyers connect timing →
consequence[22] → *risk.*

8. Core Prioritize Questions

Use **three to five** of these questions—never all—to help the buyer surface timing reality on their own.

If This Waits (Consequence Questions)

- "What happens if nothing changes this quarter?"
- "Who feels the impact first if this slips?"
- "What gets harder or more expensive the longer this stays unresolved?"
- "Which teams will feel this next, even if they're not involved today?"

If This Moves Now (Opportunity Questions)

- "What becomes easier or more stable if this is addressed now?"
- "Which risks stop showing up once this is under control?"
- "What would your team be able to focus on sooner?"

How Leadership Sees the Timing (Leadership Timing Questions)

- "When does leadership usually look at this?"
- "What planning or reporting cycles does this run into?"
- "What changes if this becomes part of next quarter instead of this one?"

These questions don't create urgency. They make timing visible.

---

22. Forrester, 2021 – buyers underestimate cost of delay unless guided.

9. Stage Transition: How You Know Prioritize Is Complete

Move to Mobilize only when the buyer demonstrates that urgency has become internally meaningful.

Look for signals such as the buyer doing the following:

- Verbalizing the cost of waiting in their own words
- Connecting consequences directly to timing
- Referencing leadership cycles ("We need this before FY planning.")
- Expressing discomfort with delay ("We can't push this again.")
- Asking implementation or sequencing questions

If these signals are absent, do not advance. Stay in Prioritize until the buyer feels the timeline clearly.

10. Mastering Stage 6—Prioritize

These exercises help you sharpen your ability to surface timing clarity without pressure. Prioritization becomes far more natural when you practice revealing the buyer's real timeline, the cost of delay, and the opportunity window that opens when action is taken now.

1. **Identify one deal that stalled because the buyer kept delaying**, and map the actual timeline they were operating under—leadership rhythms, planning cycles, downstream dependencies, and hidden constraints.
2. **Write three questions that expose the cost of waiting,** without manufacturing urgency or using emotional pressure. Focus on questions that illuminate consequences the buyer already feels but has not yet articulated.
3. **Map an opportunity window for one ICP segment:** describe what becomes possible sooner—or with less effort—when the issue is solved now rather than later.
4. **Draft one "non-pressure timeline" question**, such as:

"When will leadership revisit this topic next?" Questions like this reveal timing reality without sounding like a closing tactic.

5. **Write one dialogue line where the buyer discovers urgency themselves**, expressing the insight in their own words. Your goal is to practice facilitating realization, not delivering it.

ADVANCED PRIORITIZE

*For enterprise, multi-team, technical,
or political environments*

Advanced Prioritization

Advanced Prioritize is not about accelerating the deal. **It is about revealing the real timeline the buyer is already operating on—operationally, strategically, and politically.** Most buyers misjudge their own timing because they evaluate decisions through personal bandwidth ("*Do I have time now?*") rather than organizational reality ("*What timelines are already in motion whether I act or not?*").

When you surface those hidden timelines—quarterly capacity constraints, leadership risk reviews, planning cycles, regulatory windows, seasonal demand curves—you are not creating urgency; you are clarifying it. Buyers suddenly see that inaction is not neutral. It is a decision with a cost curve.

This shift is profound: the buyer stops asking, "*Should we do this now?*" and starts asking, "*Can we afford not to?*"

The founder's role at this stage is to illuminate the external clocks that govern the buyer's world, not introduce pressure. Your job is to help them see the true markers that will shape success or failure: when the downstream consequences will arrive, when leadership attention peaks, when competing initiatives collide, and when windows of opportunity quietly close.

When buyers see those timelines clearly, movement becomes the rational, low-risk path—not a response to persuasion.

The Consequence Ladder

A structured way to escalate timing consequences without pressure

Most buyers underestimate the cost of waiting because they experience the problem locally, not systemically. The Consequence Ladder helps them climb from *local inconvenience* to *strategic impact*—at their own pace. Each rung expands awareness without emotional manipulation.

Step 1 – Local Pain
"Who feels this first?"
Buyers see the immediate friction: delays, rework, instability.

Step 2 – Cross-Team Ripple
"Who else is affected by this?"
They begin to notice hidden workload, escalation chains, and secondary effects.

Step 3 – Operational Impact
"What slows down or breaks when this happens?"
The buyer now connects the issue to throughput, reliability, predictability, or customer experience.

Step 4 – Strategic Consequence
"What commitments get delayed or derailed?"
This is where the problem becomes a business risk—not just an operational nuisance.

Step 5 – Leadership Impact
"What will executives question if this continues?"
The buyer recognizes the political consequences: scrutiny, budget risk, trust erosion, accountability questions.

The brilliance of the ladder is its neutrality. Clarity increases with every step. Pressure never enters the conversation.

To make these timing consequences visible, here's the Consequence Ladder I use to reveal how delay creates escalating impact.

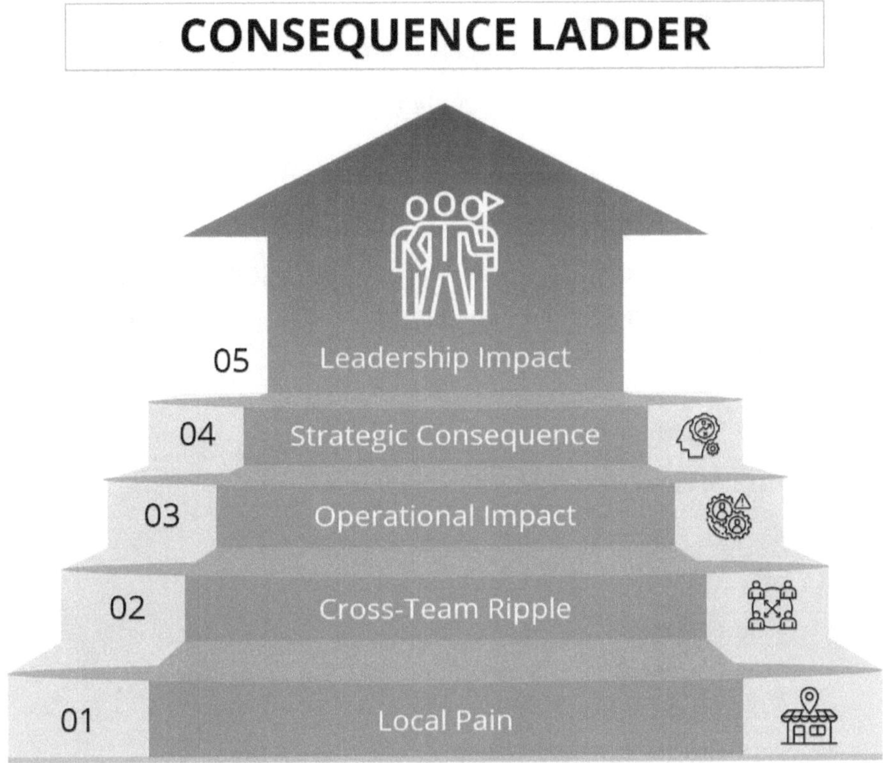

Figure 7: The Consequence Ladder

Figure 7 shows how a single problem escalates over time—from local friction to leadership-level risk—when its consequences are traced through the organization. Each rung represents a wider scope of impact, helping buyers recognize that delay is not neutral, but increasingly costly. The ladder allows prioritization to emerge through clarity rather than pressure.

The Prioritization Map

The tool executives use (without realizing it) to decide what gets attention now

Enterprise prioritization is governed by three forces: consequence, opportunity, and timing. Buyers rarely integrate all three—founders help them do so.

1. Consequence of Delay

What worsens? Who absorbs it? What becomes harder, riskier, or more expensive later? This reveals the *negative* timeline already unfolding.

2. Opportunity Window

What becomes possible sooner if the problem is solved now rather than next quarter? This surfaces the *positive* timeline—gains, not just avoided losses.

3. Timing Anchors

Every enterprise lives inside fixed cycles:

- Budget windows
- Planning cycles
- Risk reviews
- Audit seasons
- Compliance deadlines
- Customer renewal waves
- Reporting periods

Most buyers don't consciously connect their problem to these cycles. Prioritization makes that connection explicit.

Your job is not to create urgency. Your job is to *reveal the urgency that already exists.*

Dialogue Scene: Leadership Timing & the Priority Window

Isabela is a founder selling into security leadership.

CISO: I agree this needs fixing, but leadership wants to revisit priorities next quarter.

Founder (Isabela): Totally understand. Out of curiosity—when is your next risk review?

CISO: In six weeks.

Isabela: And if this issue is still unresolved during that review . . . what will leadership say?

CISO: (*pauses*) They'll ask why we didn't address it earlier.

Isabela: So the real timeline isn't next quarter—it's six weeks.

In that moment, the buyer stops operating on the imagined timeline and shifts to the *actual* one.

Buyer Psychology:
Buyers often misjudge timing inside their organization. You help them see it clearly.

Founder Story: Lana and the Operational Clock

Lana is a founder selling into operational leadership.

Lana met with a COO whose team suffered repeated machine downtime.

COO: We'll fix the process eventually. Just not this quarter.

Lana didn't push. She illuminated the timeline.

Lana: How much downtime did you absorb last quarter?

COO: Sixty-two hours.

Lana: And how much capacity does each hour cost?

COO: €12,000.

Lana: So waiting one quarter costs about €744,000 in avoidable loss?

Silence.

In that moment, the COO didn't feel pressured. He felt informed—and accountable.

Urgency wasn't emotional. It was mathematical.

The deal closed in seventeen days.

Petra's Insight:
Urgency appears when buyers connect timing to consequences—not when founders push timelines.

STAGE 7 – MOBILIZE

Champion the Initiative • Support the Buyer • Win the Internal Ecosystem

1. Psychology of Mobilize

Mobilize[23] is the final stage of the Buyer Sense system—and paradoxically, the stage where most deals collapse. Up to this point, you and the buyer have traveled far together. They understand the true problem. They have internalized the Reframe. They see the consequences of waiting. They believe in the direction. They want to move.

But wanting is not the same as winning.

The buyer now transitions from **individual cognition** to **organizational navigation**—a shift well-documented in organizational psychology and political behavior research. Scholars like Weick,[24] Pfeffer,[25] and Simon[26] have repeatedly shown

---

23. Mobilize focuses on equipping internal champions with language and structure they can use inside their organization. Research on sensemaking and framing shows that decisions stall less when stakeholders can explain both the problem and the path forward with confidence, especially in politically complex environments.

24. Karl E. Weick, *Sensemaking in Organizations* (Thousand Oaks, CA: Sage Publications, 1995).

25. Jeffrey Pfeffer, *Managing with Power: Politics and Influence in Organizations* (Boston: Harvard Business School Press, 1992).

26. Herbert A. Simon, *Administrative Behavior: A Study of Decision-Making Processes in Administrative Organizations*, 4th ed. (New York: Free Press, 1997; original work published 1947)

that people inside large systems do not make decisions alone; they make decisions *inside webs of incentives, risk perceptions, identity, and social approval.*

This is the moment when the buyer must enter that system on your behalf. Their task is no longer simply to understand—it is to **champion**, **defend**, and **sell** the insight to people who were never part of your conversations.

They must now do the following:

- Translate your Reframe into their organization's political language
- Anticipate objections from teams whose incentives differ
- Neutralize risk perceptions and turf concerns
- Position the problem in a way leadership cannot ignore
- Carry a narrative upward, sideways, and across the company

If they fail at any of these, the deal dies,[27] out of sight—not from disagreement, but from **internal gravity**, the quiet force that pulls every new initiative back toward the status quo.

This is why the final stage is not about closing. It is about **equipping**.

Buyer Psychology
A buyer becomes a champion only when they feel supported, equipped, protected, and confident navigating their internal world. No champion fights alone.

Buyers don't buy alone—they fight internal battles. Here's what their world really looks like.

---

27. Gartner, 2023 – 43% of deals stall during internal consensus-building.

MOBILIZE CHAMPION MAP

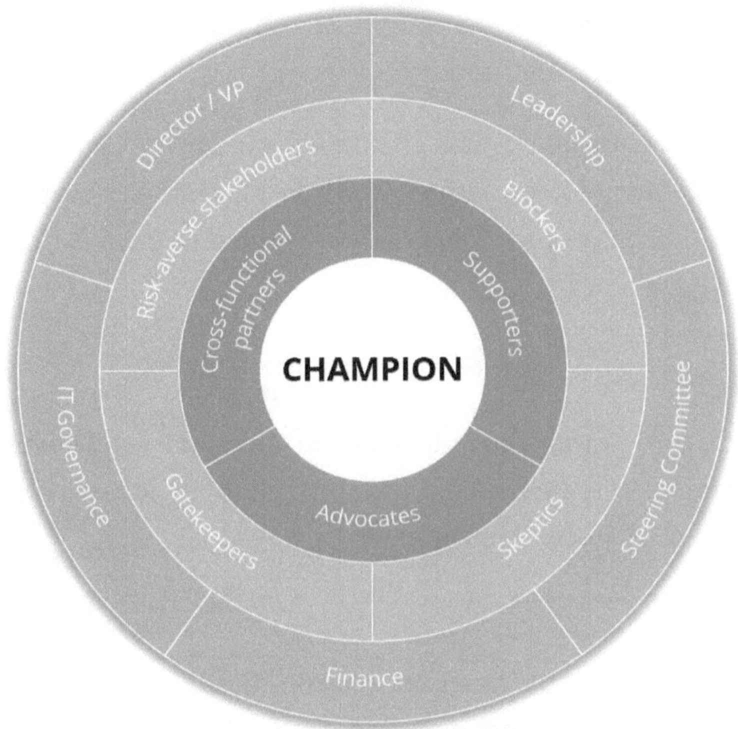

Figure 8: Mobilize Champion Map

How to Read the Mobilize Champion Map

This map shows what happens once a decision leaves your conversation and enters the organization. At this stage, the buyer must act as a champion—carrying the Reframe, navigating internal politics, anticipating resistance, and defending the decision across stakeholders without the founder present.

The **inner green ring** reflects behavior toward the initiative: **advocates** actively promote it, **supporters** agree but remain passive, and **skeptics** are unconvinced but influenceable. The **middle beige ring** reflects organizational roles: **blockers** can delay or stop progress, **gatekeepers** control the process and access, and

risk-averse stakeholders focus on avoiding blame rather than creating change. The **outer ring** represents common functions where these roles typically appear (Finance, IT Governance, Leadership, Steering Committees, etc.).

This is not an org chart—it is an influence map. Mobilize succeeds when the champion understands where support, resistance, and risk will surface—and is prepared to address each before the initiative stalls.

2. Purpose of Mobilize

Mobilize turns an aligned individual into a **system-level champion**. Your goal is to create the conditions for your buyer to win *internal conversations you will never attend.*

This requires:

- A narrative they can deliver confidently
- Objections mapped and neutralized before they appear
- Political dynamics surfaced instead of ignored
- Timing windows understood
- Roles and responsibilities clarified
- A sense of partnership, not pressure

Mobilize is the point where your buyer stops being "someone interested in a solution" and becomes **the internal owner of the initiative**.

By the end of this stage, the buyer should experience a distinct internal shift:

"I'm not just convinced—I'm ready to champion this, and I know exactly how to win."

3. What Great Sounds Like

Great mobilization feels strategic, grounded, calm, and co-creative. It sounds like two leaders shaping a change effort—not a seller preparing a pitch.

Skilled founders do the following:

- Co-build the internal narrative
- Anticipate objections before the buyer encounters them
- Help map internal influence and decision paths
- Reduce social and political risk
- Equip the buyer with clarity, confidence, and language

In practice, great mobilization creates a **decision support structure**—a shared way of thinking that helps the buyer navigate uncertainty and interpersonal risk. You are effectively giving them a stronger architecture for influence.

This is what creates real champions.

4. What Bad Sounds Like

Poor mobilization is defined by abandonment—the founder assumes the buyer will "take it from here."

This typically includes the following:

- Sending a deck instead of building a narrative
- Ignoring internal politics
- Assuming the buyer knows what to say
- Leaving objections unaddressed
- Overloading with detail instead of clarifying the story
- Asking for a decision instead of preparing the champion

Bad mobilization forces the buyer into a fragile position: advocating for something without the clarity or political coverage to do so effectively.

Deals do not die from rejection. They die from **internal overwhelm**.

5. Common Founder Mistakes in Mobilize

Most founders underestimate the social and political work required to move an initiative through a real organization. They mistakenly assume the following:

- If the buyer "gets it," everyone else will too.
- If one person is aligned, the system must be aligned.
- If the value is clear, objections won't appear.
- If they send materials, the buyer can sell it.
- If they push, momentum increases.

In reality:

Most deals fail not because the buyer disagrees—but because the buyer **cannot win internally**.

6. Business Reality: Where Mobilize Lives

Mobilize sits at the intersection of five forces well-documented in decision science[28]:

1. Internal Politics

Influence networks, turf conflicts, ego protection, and status dynamics.

2. Functional Priorities

Each department carries its own worldview: efficiency, risk, growth, compliance, brand, or capacity.

---

28. For decisionscience foundations on how politics, functional lenses, timing constraints, risk perceptions, and champion efficacy shape organizational decisions, see Kahneman & Tversky (2000); Bazerman & Moore (2012); Pfeffer (1992); Cyert & March (1963); Mintzberg et al. (1976); Tversky & Kahneman (1991); Bandura (1997).

3. Leadership Timing Windows

Budget cycles, strategic planning, board reviews, and risk assessments—all shape when decisions can and cannot be made.

4. Perceived Risk vs. Reward

People are more motivated to avoid blame than to pursue improvement.

5. Champion Readiness

A buyer with conviction but without confidence cannot carry the initiative forward.

Founders who understand this become indispensable. Founders who ignore it disappear from the deal.

7. Mini-Dialogue Example: Preparing the Buyer to Win the Internal Meeting

Founder (Michael): Who will you need to bring this to internally?

VP Product: Engineering, definitely. And our CTO.

Michael: What will Engineering push back on?

VP Product: Capacity. They'll say they don't have time.

Michael: And your CTO—what matters most to them?

VP Product: Predictability. It's becoming a board-level issue.

Michael: Great. Let's build a one-page narrative that speaks directly to both. You won't need to convince them—you'll just need to guide them.

Champions don't need persuasion.
They need **preparation**.

8. Core Mobilize Questions

The following questions are not tactics—they are strategic scaffolding used to help the buyer map the internal ecosystem and prepare to win within it.

Who Carries Weight (Champion Identity)

- "Whose perspective tends to shape decisions once discussions start?"
- "Who do people look to when there's disagreement?"

Where Alignment Breaks (Internal Dynamics)

- "Where do you expect questions or hesitation to come up?"
- "Who needs to be involved early so this doesn't stall later?"

How the Story Lands (Narrative Clarity)

- "How do you think leadership will hear this when it's first raised?"
- "What would help you feel confident walking into that conversation?"

These questions build readiness and confidence—not urgency.

9. Stage Transition: How You Know Mobilize Is Complete

A deal is ready to move only when the buyer demonstrates **internal readiness**, not just personal agreement.

Look for these signs:

- They can articulate the Reframe in their own internal language.
- They can defend the logic clearly and calmly.
- They have a simple narrative, not a deck.
- They know who to talk to, in what order, and why.
- They feel prepared for objections.

- They express confidence and ownership. ("I'm ready to take this forward.")

If even one of these is missing, you are *not* at the close stage yet.

10. Mastering Stage 7—Mobilize

Use this exercise to help your buyer become a confident internal champion—one who can navigate politics, objections, and leadership expectations with clarity.

1. Map every stakeholder in their internal ecosystem and note their likely stance, influence, and concerns.
2. Draft a one-page internal narrative your champion can deliver without modification.
3. List predictable objections by function, and write the neutral, logic-based responses that defuse each one.
4. Identify political blockers and outline strategies to mitigate or bypass them.
5. Prepare a concise "leadership interpretation statement" that frames the initiative in executive language.
6. Write the exact opening sentence your champion can use to begin their internal pitch with confidence.

What Mobilize Looks Like in Practice

Context:
A VP of Product agrees with the Reframe but must take it to Engineering, Finance, and the CTO.

Stakeholder Map (simplified):

- Engineering: Worried about capacity and scope changes
- Finance: Focused on cost predictability
- CTO: Concerned with delivery reliability and board scrutiny

Shared Internal Narrative: "This isn't a speed or capacity issue. It's a commitment stability issue caused by late-stage approval changes."

Predictable Objection (Engineering): "We're already overloaded."

Neutral Response: "The overload comes from rework after priorities shift—not from planned work."

Leadership Interpretation Statement: "This initiative reduces delivery risk by stabilizing decisions before work begins."

Champion Opening Line: "I want to explain why our missed commitments aren't an execution problem—and what's actually driving them."

ADVANCED MOBILIZE

(For enterprise, multi-team, political,
or high-stakes environments)

Mobilization is where the deal is ultimately decided. At this stage, the buyer's challenge is no longer analytical—it is organizational. Decades of research in organizational behavior and decision science show that choices in complex institutions do not arise from individual judgment alone. They are shaped by **interdependent incentives, social approval, political constraints, and collective sensemaking processes.**[29, 30, 31]

This is the landscape your champion must navigate—a landscape governed not by logic, but by **organizational forces**. Your role is to equip them to move confidently and effectively within it.

Use this section as a preparation sequence: identify your champion's archetype first, then complete the Mobilization Map, and finish by co-writing the one-page internal narrative they will use in stakeholder meetings.

---

29. March, James G., and Johan P. Olsen. *Rediscovering Institutions* (1989).

30. Mintzberg, Henry. *Power In and Around Organizations.* Englewood Cliffs, NJ: Prentice-Hall, 1983.

31. Cyert, Richard M., and James G. March. *A Behavioral Theory of the Firm.* Englewood Cliffs, NJ: Prentice-Hall, 1963.

The Three Mobilizer Archetypes

Every buyer who becomes a champion does so through a dominant mode of influence. Some win through logic, some through political safety, and others through operational credibility.

These archetypes are not personality labels—they describe **how a buyer earns internal trust and moves decisions forward**. Identifying which archetype you're working with tells you exactly **what kind of narrative, evidence, and support they will need to succeed internally**—and what will cause them to stall if it's missing.

Every champion navigates their organization differently. Identifying their archetype determines how you must prepare them:

1. The Analyst Champion

Structured thinkers who need logic, clarity, and crisp internal argumentation.
They win by helping decision-makers *understand*.

2. The Political Champion

Highly attuned to influence, alliances, and narrative framing.
They win by helping people *feel safe*.

3. The Operational Champion

Practical executors who care about predictability, workflow stability, and team impact. They win by helping leaders *trust feasibility*.

Knowing the archetype tells you exactly what narrative, tools, and evidence this person must carry into the internal room.

The Mobilization Map

Once the archetype is clear, the Mobilization Map helps you prepare the champion for the specific internal terrain they must navigate.

The following is a four-part tool for preparing a champion to fight and win internally:

1. Stakeholder Map

Who must be **informed**, **consulted**, **aligned**, **reassured**, or **neutralized**? This reveals the true decision coalition—not the org chart.

2. Pushback Forecast

Predictable objections by function:

- Engineering → capacity or technical debt
- Finance → stability, predictability, cost certainty
- Ops → disruption, workload
- Leadership → timing, strategic risk, optics

Forecasting these removes surprise and builds confidence.

3. Internal Dynamics

Uncover the forces that shape internal decisions:

- Incentive structures
- Legacy tensions
- Psychological safety
- Political sensitivities
- Competing priorities

This is the reality your champion must navigate.

4. The Confidence Path

What the champion must know, feel, and be able to articulate before going into the internal meeting. Confidence is not a trait—it is a *state* created through preparation.

Internal Narrative Template (One-Page Case)

This template exists to replace slides, opinions, and fragmented explanations with a **shared internal story that holds under scrutiny**. Its purpose is not to sell, persuade, or impress—but to help the champion **explain the problem and direction consistently**, regardless of audience, politics, or pushback. When done well, this one page becomes the buyer's anchor in meetings you will never attend.

Champions rarely win by presenting decks. They win by presenting **clarity on a single page**. This page should include the following:

1. **Problem summary** – the Reframe stated cleanly
2. **Evidence** – decoded workflow insights
3. **Risk of delay** – consequences of inaction
4. **Opportunity** – what becomes possible sooner
5. **Solution type** – the category that solves the root cause
6. **Strategic fit** – alignment with leadership priorities

This becomes the internal narrative your champion can carry into conversations you will never attend.

Dialogue Scene: Buyer Makes the Internal Pitch

CTO: Why are we looking at this now?

VP Product: Because our issue isn't velocity—it's predictability.

CTO: What's causing that?

VP Product: Unstable intake. Engineering isn't the bottleneck—upstream is.

CTO: And the consequence?

VP Product: Missed commitments and rising leadership scrutiny.

CTO: Why this approach?

VP Product: Because it stabilizes intake—the true root cause.

This is Mobilize done well: a champion who can articulate, defend, and win the internal debate.

Political Risk Radar

In enterprise environments, political variables can outweigh technical ones.
Identify blockers early:

- *Silent objectors*
- *Competing initiatives*
- *Resource guardians*
- *Status quo protectors*
- *Leadership sensitivities*
- *Cross-functional tensions*

Political friction kills deals faster than product limitations.

The Champion Confidence Ladder

Your job is to move the champion step by step:

Level 1 – Understands the problem
Level 2 – Believes the Reframe
Level 3 – Can explain it
Level 4 – Can justify it
Level 5 – Can move it forward internally

Most deals stall between Levels 3 and 4.
Elite founders guide champions to Level 5.

Founder Story: Luca and the Internal Battlefield

Luca is a founder working in complex enterprise environments.

Luca worked with a retail CISO who fully understood the Reframe—but the internal ecosystem did not.

- Architecture feared integration debt.
- Finance questioned cost predictability.
- Leadership believed the timing was too tight.

Instead of pushing the CISO to "sell harder," Luca said: "Let's build the internal case together—team by team."

They crafted:

- A technical validation brief for Architecture
- A risk-reduction summary for leadership
- A cost-stability model for Finance

When the CISO walked into the executive meeting, he entered fully equipped, confident, and credible.

He closed the deal for her. That is the power of Mobilize.

FOUNDER PLAYBOOK SUMMARY

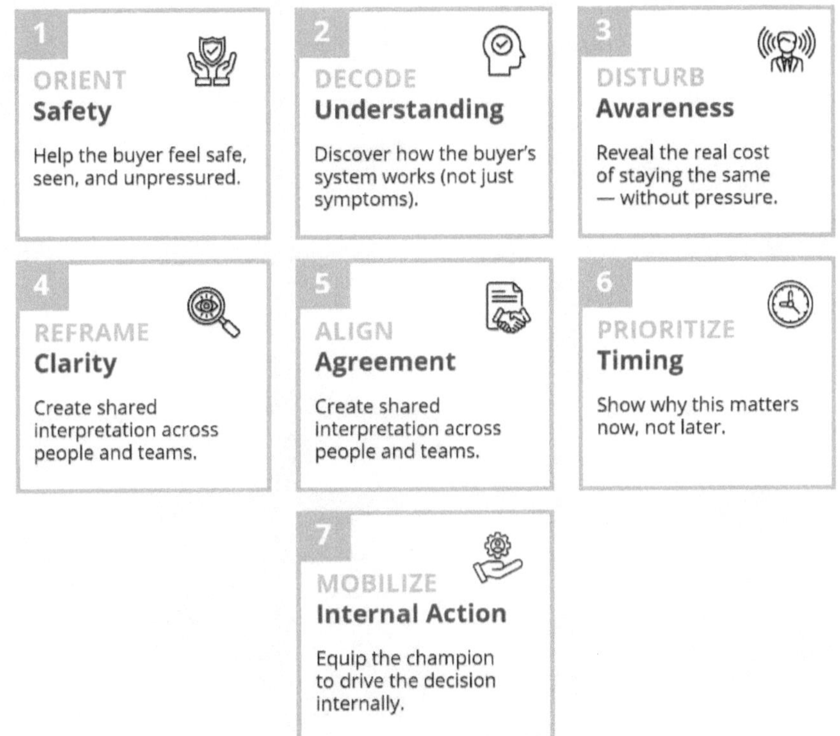

Figure 9: Founder Playbook Summary

This figure 9 summarizes what the founder must equip the champion with to mobilize the organization: the stakeholder landscape, predictable objections, internal dynamics, and a clear confidence path. It acts as a practical checklist—so the buyer doesn't just agree in the meeting, but can defend and advance the decision after the meeting.

PART III

APPLICATION & TOOLS

Part III exists to turn understanding into execution. The stages you've learned are not something to memorize—they are something to *recognize and navigate in real time*. The tools in this section are designed to help you do exactly that, without turning Buyer Sense into a script or a rigid process.

HOW TO USE PART III – APPLICATION & TOOLS

Part III is where Buyer Sense Conversations moves from understanding to **application**.

In Parts I and II, you learned:

- Why modern buyers struggle with overload, internal politics, and the fear of being wrong
- How the Buyer Sense flow works
  (*Orient* → *Decode* → *Disturb* → *Reframe* → *Align* → *Prioritize* → *Mobilize*)
- How buying decisions actually move internally
  (*Interpret* → *Align* → *Defend*)

Part III is designed to help you **use** all of that in real conversations.

This is not a section you read once and move on from. It is a **working part of the book**—something you return to before calls, after calls, during deal reviews, and whenever something feels stuck or unclear.

How Part III Is Structured

Part III contains **two different types of content**, each with a distinct role:

1. Assets — what you *use*

Assets are practical reference materials: examples, questions, tools, and templates. They are meant to be revisited, printed, and applied directly in real deals.

You will find four assets in Part III:

- **Asset 1 — Buyer Sense Conversations: Quick Examples (p. 187)**
- **Asset 2 — Buyer Sense Conversations: Full Transcript (p. 190)**
- **Asset 3 — The Sensemaking Question Library (p. 197)**
- **Asset 4 — Buyer Sense Tools & Templates (p. 229)**

These assets are not meant to be consumed sequentially. Use them based on the situation you are in.

2. Sections — how you *build skill*

The seven sections in Part III provide guidance, practice structure, diagnostics, and integration.

They explain **how and when** to use the assets—and how to turn Buyer Sense into a repeatable habit and, eventually, a leadership skill.

The sections are:

- **Section 1 — Putting Buyer Sense into Practice (p. 219)**
- **Section 2 — Practice Rhythms & Habits (p. 223)**
- **Section 3 — Using the Buyer Sense Playbook (p. 229)**
- **Section 4 — Buyer Sense Failure Modes (p. 235)**
- **Section 5 — Using Buyer Sense Tools (p. 241)**
- **Section 6 — Using Buyer Sense Templates (p. 243)**
- **Section 7 — Final Reflection: Becoming a Buyer Sensemaker (p. 247)**

These sections help you move from *knowing* the framework to *embodying* it.

How to Navigate Part III (Quick Paths)

You do not need to master everything at once. Most founders come to Part III with a **specific situation**. We have listed some common situations below to help you get started:

"I have a call coming up. I need clarity fast."

Go to:

- **Asset 1 — Buyer Sense Conversations: Quick Examples (p. 187)**
- **Asset 4 — Buyer Sense Tools & Templates** (*Playbook + Pre-Call tools*) **(p. 229)**

Use these to enter the call calm, structured, and grounded—without scripting yourself.

"I need better questions, not better pitches."

Go to:

- **Asset 3 — The Sensemaking Question Library (p. 197)**

Select a few questions for the stage you are in. Let the buyer's answers determine the direction.

"Our deals keep stalling internally."

Go to:

- **Asset 4 — Buyer Sense Tools & Templates** (*Align, Prioritize, Mobilize tools*) **(p. 229)**
- **Section 4 — Buyer Sense Failure Modes (p. 235)**

Your role here is not persuasion—it is equipping the buyer to win internal conversations.

"I want this to become a consistent practice, not a one-off idea."

Go to:

- **Section 1 — Putting** Buyer Sense into Practice (p. 219)
- **Section 2 — Practice Rhythms & Habits** (p. 223)

These sections show how to build Buyer Sense into your weekly workflow without overwhelm.

"Something feels off in my conversations, but I can't name it."

Go to:

- **Section 4 — Buyer Sense Failure Modes (p. 235)**

Use it as a diagnostic tool. Identify the failure mode, apply the fix, and restore the flow.

"I want this to shape who I am as a founder."

Go to:

- **Section 7 — Final Reflection: Becoming a Buyer Sensemaker (p. 247)**

This is where Buyer Sense becomes a leadership identity—not just a sales method.

A Final Note

You don't need to use everything in Part III at once.

- **Before calls** → Assets 1, 3, and 4
- **After calls** → Sections 4, 5, and 6
- **Weekly** → Section 2
- **Over time** → Section 7

Buyer Sense Conversations is not about pressure or performance. It is about bringing clarity into complex buyer environments.

Part III is where you learn to do that—calmly, consistently, and with confidence.

Asset 1—Buyer Sense Conversations – Quick Examples

This asset gives you **fast pattern recognition**.

The Quick Examples show the full seven-stage Buyer Sense flow inside a single conversation—without explanation, theory, or commentary. Each stage appears once, in sequence, so you can see how Orient, Decode, Disturb, Reframe, Align, Prioritize, and Mobilize sound when they work together naturally.

Use this asset when:

- You want a **mental reset before a call**
- You're learning the flow for the first time
- You want to check *where you are* versus *where you should go next*

Do not analyze these examples line by line. Read them as **flow**, **tone**, and **direction**—then move into your call with that rhythm in mind.

One-Page SaaS Example

Before we dive into the detailed transcripts, here are quick examples that show the seven-stage flow in real calls:

Stage 1 – Orient

Rob: Thanks for making the time. I reviewed your Q1 initiative notes so we can stay focused. Here's what I propose . . . First, I'd love to understand how your current release workflow works today. Second, if helpful, I can share patterns we see. Third, we can decide together if it makes sense to go deeper.

VP Product: Appreciate the prep.

Stage 2 – Decode

Rob: Walk me through your current cycle.

Ops lead: It changes. Some weeks Engineering is the bottleneck, some weeks QA.

Rob: And when it changes unpredictably?

Ops lead: It kills sprint planning.

Stage 3 – Disturb

Rob: Unpredictable bottlenecks usually point to upstream reliability issues, not team capacity.

VP Product: That . . . hits home.

Stage 4 – Reframe

Rob: You don't have a velocity issue. You have a predictability issue. Fix predictability → velocity improves.

Engineering manager: Exactly.

Stage 5 – Align

Rob: If predictability is the real root cause, dashboards won't solve it. Stabilizing intake will.

VP Product: That aligns with how we've been thinking.

Stage 6 – Prioritize

Rob: If nothing changes, what happens in Q3?

VP Product: More unpredictability.

Stage 7 – Mobilize

Rob: Here's a one-page summary for your CTO with risks and framing.

VP Product: Great—let's bring them into the next call.

One-Page Manufacturing Example

Stage 1 – Orient (Opening)

Founder: Before we dive in, what would make this conversation valuable for you?

Plant manager: Clarity. We've had throughput issues for months.

Stage 2 – Decode (Understanding the System)

Founder: Walk me through what happens when a line slows unexpectedly.

Plant manager: Operators jump in manually.

Stage 3 – Disturb (Revealing Hidden Downstream Effects)

Founder: And when operators intervene manually, what gets delayed downstream?

Plant manager: Quality checks. And then rework piles up.

Stage 4 – Reframe (Mental Model Shift)

Founder: So this isn't downtime—it's capacity reliability.

COO: . . . that actually fits what we're seeing.

Stage 5 – Align (Bringing Teams to Shared Interpretation)

Founder: How would Engineering describe this issue?

COO: As equipment inconsistency. Finance says overtime.

Stage 6 – Prioritize (Clarifying Timing & Consequences)

Founder: What happens if nothing changes this quarter?

COO: We'll miss the delivery window for our largest customer.

Stage 7 – Mobilize (Preparing the Internal Case)

Founder: Let's build a one-page brief you can take to Leadership to align the story.

Asset 2—Buyer Sense Conversations – Full Transcript

This asset is about **depth, pacing, and transitions**.

The transcript in this chapter shows a complete Buyer Sense conversation in its entirety—uncompressed and realistic. You will see pauses, follow-ups, clarification, and subtle shifts between stages. Nothing is optimized for performance or scripted for effect.

This is what a real conversation looks like when a founder **guides buyer sensemaking instead of pushing decisions**.

Use this asset when:

- You want to study how Buyer Sense stages unfold over time
- You're unsure how to move from one stage to the next
- You want to see how urgency is created without pressure

Read this transcript slowly. Pay attention not just to *what* is asked, but *when* it is asked—and what changes inside the room before the conversation advances.

Buyer Sense Conversation – *Reducing Call Volume Without Ripping the Stack*

A Founder–CIO Conversation in a Mid-Size Retail Bank

Setting

A founder is meeting with the CIO of a mid-size retail bank. The bank has been investing heavily in digital transformation but continues to struggle with high call center volumes and inconsistent customer experience across channels.

The founder's company offers an AI-powered customer service platform designed to integrate with existing systems rather than replace them.

The Conversation

Founder:
Thanks for making the time. I know you're getting pitched constantly, so I want to make this conversation genuinely useful. Before we dive in—what's been the most frustrating part of scaling customer service at the bank?

CIO:
Honestly? Fragmentation. We've got legacy systems, a chatbot that doesn't really understand context, and agents juggling five different tools. It's clunky.

Founder:
That sounds painful. When that fragmentation shows up, where does it hurt the most—on the customer side or internally?

CIO:
Both. Customers get bounced around. Internally, we're seeing high attrition in the call center. No one wants to deal with angry callers all day.

Founder:
Makes sense. And when you think about fixing that, what's the business case you'd need to justify a change? Is it cost savings, NPS, retention?

CIO:
All of the above. But realistically, I'd need to show a reduction in call volume and some hard savings within six to twelve months.

Founder:

Got it. We built our platform for exactly that kind of environment—messy tech stacks, pressure to reduce volume, and pressure to improve experience at the same time. Before I go any further, are you already evaluating other vendors?

CIO:

A few. Most are either too light or want us to rip out half our stack.

Founder:

Yeah, we see that a lot. Our approach was to sit on top of what you already have—legacy cores, CRM, even your IVR. If I showed you how another regional bank reduced call volume by 32% in nine months using that approach, would that be relevant?

CIO:

It would. But I'd want to understand how much lift it took to get there.

Founder:

Fair. It took them six weeks to go live. We started with one use case—fraud claims—and expanded from there. If it makes sense, I can walk you through that in a working session with your head of Operations.

CIO:

Yeah. Let's do that. Bring the team in.

This is a buyer-led conversation. The founder does not pitch features. They diagnose, align on business impact, and only then position their solution.

That is Buyer Sense in practice.

Explaining the Conversation Through the Buyer Sense Lens

Let's walk through the founder–CIO conversation again, this time mapped explicitly to the **Buyer Sense stages**. This will show how each part of the dialogue aligns with how buyers actually move through decisions—not how sellers wish they would.

1. Orient

Founder:
"Thanks for making the time. I know you're getting pitched constantly, so I want to make this conversation genuinely useful. Before we dive in—what's been the most frustrating part of scaling customer service at the bank?"

The founder opens with respect and clarity. There is no pitch, no positioning, and no attempt to sound impressive.

This creates **psychological safety** and sets a tone of mutual exploration. The buyer understands that this conversation is about making sense of their situation—not being sold to.

2. Decode

CIO:
"Honestly? Fragmentation. We've got legacy systems, a chatbot that doesn't really understand context, and agents juggling five different tools."

Founder:
"That sounds painful. When that fragmentation shows up, where does it hurt the most—on the customer side or internally?"

Here, the founder helps the CIO unpack the current state.

Instead of accepting "fragmentation" as a generic problem statement, the founder asks where it shows up most. This is

Decode in action—turning surface symptoms into concrete, observable consequences inside the system.

3. Disturb

CIO:
"Both. Customers get bounced around. Internally, we're seeing high attrition in the call center."

Founder:
"Makes sense. And when you think about fixing that, what's the business case you'd need to justify a change?"

This question gently introduces **stakes.**

It's not fear-based and it's not confrontational. Instead, it surfaces:

- The cost of inaction
- What would need to be true for the buyer to move forward safely

Disturb is not about creating urgency. It's about clarifying what matters.

4. Reframe

Founder:
"We built our platform for exactly that kind of environment—messy tech stacks, pressure to reduce volume, and pressure to improve experience at the same time."

Here, the founder Reframes the problem from **"fragmented systems"** to **"operating under pressure to reduce volume and improve experience in a messy environment."**

This shifts the lens from technology to business reality. The buyer is no longer evaluating tools—they are reconsidering how the problem itself should be understood.

5. Align

CIO:

"Most vendors either feel too light or want us to rip out half our stack."

Founder:

"Ours was built to sit on top of what you already have—legacy cores, CRM, even your IVR."

This part addresses **internal alignment.**

The founder demonstrates awareness of:

- IT constraints
- operational risk
- internal resistance

By respecting those constraints, the founder avoids triggering defensiveness from IT, operations, or architecture teams that are not even in the room yet.

6. Prioritize

Founder:

"If I showed you how another regional bank reduced call volume by 32% in nine months, would that be relevant?"

CIO:

"It would. But I'd want to understand how much lift it took to get there."

Now the founder begins to **build urgency through credibility.**

The buyer is no longer asking whether the problem matters. They are weighing **effort, feasibility, and timing**—a clear signal that this has become a real priority.

7. Mobilize

Founder:
"We started with one use case—fraud claims—and expanded from there. I could walk you through that in a working session with your head of operations."

CIO:
"Yeah. Let's bring the team in."

This is the **mobilization moment.**

The founder does not push for a close. Instead, they set up the next step that enables internal selling—bringing in additional stakeholders and creating shared understanding.

The buyer is now willing to move the conversation forward inside the organization.

Why This Matters

This is what Buyer Sense looks like in practice.

The founder does not:

- Rush to solutions
- Rely on persuasion
- Confuse interest with readiness

Instead, they guide the buyer through their own **clarity journey—** from confusion to alignment to action.

You're not selling. You're helping the buyer make sense of a decision they need to defend.

That's Buyer Sense.

Asset 3—The Sensemaking Question Library

This asset is a **thinking system**, not a script.

The Sensemaking Question Library helps you guide complex buyer conversations by asking questions that create clarity, surface patterns, and support internal alignment—without triggering defensiveness or pressure.

Each stage includes:

- Core questions that work in most situations
- Deeper insight and political questions
- Mini-dialogues to demonstrate tone and pacing
- Red flag → green flag corrections for common founder mistakes

Use this asset when:

- You feel stuck or uncertain in a conversation
- You notice yourself talking too much
- A buyer seems engaged but not moving forward
- Internal dynamics or politics start to surface

Choose a **few questions**, not many. Let the buyer's answers determine what comes next.

What This Library Contains

Each stage of the Buyer Sense Flow includes:

- **Core Questions**
  Reliable questions that work in nearly every conversation.
- **Insight Questions**
  Questions that reveal patterns, friction, upstream causes, and systemic issues.
- **Transition Questions**

Signals that show the current stage is complete and allow you to move forward smoothly.

- **Political and Cross-Functional Questions**
  For mapping internal dynamics without triggering resistance or defensiveness.
- **Mini-Dialogues**
  Short examples that demonstrate tone, pacing, and sequencing in a Sensemaking-style conversation.
- **Red Flag → Green Flag Corrections**
  The most common founder mistakes paired with how to correct them immediately.

With these elements, you know **what to ask, when to ask it, and why it works.**

How to Use This Section

- **Before a call:**
  Select a handful of questions from the stage you expect to operate in. Use them to anchor the conversation, not to script it.
- **During a call:**
  Choose questions based on what the buyer reveals. Let their answers determine the next step.
- **After a call:**
  Review which stage you completed and what remains unfinished. Identify the next best question, not the next best pitch.
- **When you're stuck:**
  Return to the Red Flag → Green Flag section to correct tone, pacing, or sequencing.

This approach turns your conversations from reactive to intentional.

Why These Questions Work

Every question in this library is designed to:

- Create psychological safety
- Reveal truth without pressure
- Surface hidden friction
- Trigger insight, not defensiveness
- Uncover cross-functional misalignment
- Build internal alignment
- Strengthen buyer clarity and confidence
- Support champions in the internal sale
- Maintain direction without dominance

They are informed by how modern buyers think, decide, navigate politics, and move from uncertainty to action.

A Note on Sequencing

Each set of questions corresponds to a specific cognitive shift inside the Buyer Sense Flow:

- **Orient** – safety, structure, focus
- **Decode** – understanding the system
- **Disturb** – naming risks and consequences
- **Reframe** – shifting the mental model
- **Align** – bringing teams to shared interpretation
- **Prioritize** – clarifying timing and urgency
- **Mobilize** – preparing the internal case

Move to the next stage only after the buyer has completed the shift. If the conversation feels heavy, forced, or confusing, return to the **Core Questions** of the current stage.

If You Are New to Buyer Sense

Start with the essentials:

1. Read the **Core Questions** for each stage.

2. Practice the **Mini-Dialogues** to internalize tone.
3. Use **Red Flag → Green Flag** to avoid common pitfalls.
4. Add Insight and Political Questions once you feel comfortable with the fundamentals.

You do not need to master everything at once.
Progress comes from consistent practice, not memorization.

Your Advantage

Most sellers pressure buyers. Very few help them think.

When you master these questions, you become the calm, structured, trusted presence in the room—the founder who creates clarity where others create confusion.

That is the essence of a **Buyer Sensemaker.**

Stage 1 – Orient

Questions That Create Safety, Focus & Control

Orient questions set the tone. Buyers relax because they feel the founder has structure, clarity, and respect for their time. These questions prevent the call from drifting into chaos.

Core Orient Questions

- "Before we dive in, what would make this conversation valuable for you today?"
- "What was happening internally that made this topic important now?"
- "Is there anything sensitive or important we should be aware of before we go deeper?"
- "From your perspective, what does a successful outcome of this meeting look like?"
- Would it be helpful if I suggested a simple way to structure our conversation?"

Mini-Dialogue Example

Founder: Before we dive in, what would make this a great use of your time?

Buyer: Clarity. We've been dealing with conflicting signals internally.

Founder: Got it. If we use this time to sort through those signals and understand where they're coming from, would that be valuable?

Buyer: Yes, absolutely.

Red Flag → Green Flag

Red flag: "So . . . what do you want to talk about today?"

Green flag: "To make this valuable, what outcome should we aim for together?"

Red flag: "Let me pitch you our approach first."

Green flag: "Would it be helpful if I suggested a simple structure to make sure we focus on what matters most to you?"

Why These Questions Work

Orient questions work because they **reset the buyer's nervous system.**

They signal:

- **Safety** ("You won't be pressured today.")
- **Control** ("You can shape the direction.")
- **Clarity** ("You know what we're trying to accomplish together.")
- **Respect** ("Your time and context matter. I prepared for you.")

These questions disarm the natural defensiveness buyers bring into first conversations.

They shift the buyer from:

evaluation mode → collaboration mode

. . . which unlocks honest detail later in the call.

Orient questions don't extract information—they create the psychological conditions in which **the buyer willingly shares it.**

Stage 2 – Decode

Questions That Reveal Systems, Flows & Constraints

Decode questions uncover how the buyer's world actually works—their workflows, their upstream triggers, downstream consequences, manual workarounds, coordination gaps, and hidden friction. These questions turn unknowns into patterns.

System Flow Questions

- "Walk me through what happens the moment the issue begins."
- "What typically triggers this situation on a normal day?"
- "What do operators/team members do first when this happens?"
- "Who else gets pulled into the situation?"
- "Where does the problem show up first—and where does it show up last?"

Upstream/Downstream Questions

- "When this happens upstream, what breaks downstream?"
- "Who feels the strongest impact?"
- "What becomes harder because of this?"
- "What gets delayed as a result?"
- "Which teams ask you to 'fix' things that started elsewhere?"

Hidden Friction Questions

- "Where do manual workarounds happen most often?"
- "What part of this process is the most frustrating for people involved?"
- "What's something that always takes longer than it should?"
- "What gets dropped when things get busy?"
- "Which part of the workflow feels most unpredictable?"

Mini-Dialogue Example

Founder: Walk me through what happens when a line slows unexpectedly.

Supervisor: Operators jump in manually, then QC piles up.

Founder: And when QC piles up?

Supervisor: Planning loses trust in our output and starts adjusting forecasts.

Founder: So one slowdown becomes a cross-team disruption.

Red Flag → Green Flag

Red flag: "So . . . what's wrong?"

Green flag: "When this issue begins, what's the very first thing people do?"

Red flag: "Is this problem big or small?"

Green flag: "Who feels the impact strongest when this happens?"

Why These Questions Work

Decode questions work because they shift the buyer from **stories** to **systems.**

Buyers describe:

- Symptoms

- Frustrations
- Isolated incidents

Decode questions uncover how the system actually works by revealing:

- **Workflows** (what really happens, step by step)
- **Upstream triggers** (what causes the issue to start)
- **Downstream impacts** (who and what is affected later)
- **Hidden friction** (where time, effort, or value is lost)
- **Repeating patterns** (why the same problems keep coming back)

Instead of collecting anecdotes, founders gain a **map of the buyer's reality**.

- Decode works because it:
- Slows the buyer down
- Removes guesswork
- Surfaces cross-team consequences
- Builds trust through understanding

Most importantly, Decode questions help the buyer see more of their own system in five minutes than they have in five months.

This clarity creates the runway for **Disturb** and **Reframe**—the buyer must first see the system clearly before they can question it or change it.

Stage 3 – Disturb

Questions That Reveal Consequences, Tension & Hidden Risk

Disturb questions expose the real cost of the buyer's current situation. They do not pressure the buyer—they clarify reality.

Great Disturb questions help buyers see:

- Where friction starts

- Where and how it spreads
- Who carries the burden
- What becomes harder later
- What risks are underestimated
- What the downstream impact truly is

Done well, Disturb creates the moment of realization: "We can't keep doing it this way."

Consequence Questions

- *"When this happens, what's usually the first thing that starts to slip?"*
- *"Who usually gets pulled in to deal with this, even if it's not officially their responsibility?"*
- *"What does this make harder over time?"*
- *"How does this show up when you're trying to plan or forecast?"*
- *"What usually gets delayed when this comes up?"*

Risk Exposure Questions

- *"What part of this do people tend to underestimate?"*
- *"If nothing changes, what's the worst case you worry about?"*
- *"If this continues for another quarter, what starts to feel unworkable?"*
- *"How does this come up in leadership conversations?"*
- *"Where does this quietly create extra cost or wasted effort?"*

Pattern-Recognition Questions

- *"When did you first notice this becoming a pattern?"*
- *"What's been happening more often over time?"*
- *"What's showing up more now than it did last year?"*
- *"What keeps coming back no matter who tries to fix it?"*
- *"What's usually the first sign that things are about to break?"*

Mini-Dialogue Example

Founder: When QC delays stack up, what usually happens next?
Planner: Forecasts become unreliable.

Founder: And when forecasts aren't reliable, what does that do to planning?
Planner: We stop trusting the plan. People start padding timelines.

Founder: And once that happens?
Planner: Scheduling breaks. Overtime spikes. Other teams feel it.

Founder: So a small delay ends up disrupting a lot more than QC.

Red Flag → Green Flag

Red flag: "Is this a serious problem or not really?"

Green flag: "What becomes impossible if this continues for another quarter?"

Red flag: "Would you say this is annoying or critical?"

Green flag: "When this pattern repeats, who absorbs the burden?"

Why These Questions Work

Disturb questions work because they illuminate **the hidden cost of the status quo**—calmly, precisely, and without pressure.

They shift the buyer's attention from *What is happening* to *What it causes*:

- **Downstream ripple effects** (how one issue spreads across the organization)
- **Organizational friction** (where teams absorb the impact)
- **Underestimated risks** (what feels manageable until it isn't)
- **Strategic consequences** (what this blocks or limits over time)

- **The real cost of inaction** (what not changing actually costs)

Buyers rarely connect these dots on their own, because the pain is **distributed across teams, time, and decisions**.

Disturb questions assemble the whole picture. They create urgency not through emotion, but through clarity:

"We can't keep doing it this way."

That realization is what opens the door to **Reframe**.

Stage 4 – Reframe

Questions That Shift Insight, Connect Patterns & Create Mental Models

Reframe questions guide the buyer from symptom thinking to system thinking to root-cause clarity.

They help buyers *discover* the deeper truth instead of being pushed toward it.

Root-Cause Questions

These questions gently help the buyer uncover what's beneath the surface.

- *"What do you think is actually driving this?"*
- *"When this shows up in different teams, what pattern do you notice?"*
- *"What do these issues seem to have in common?"*
- *"If this issue suddenly went away, what do you think would surface next?"*
- *"Where do you think the real instability might be coming from?"*

Pattern Recognition Questions

These questions help the buyer see repeating signals and systemic dynamics.

- *"Are you seeing something similar in other parts of the company?"*
- *"When this happens, what tends to show up shortly after?"*
- *"What keeps repeating, even after people try to fix it?"*
- *"What's been happening more often over the last quarter?"*
- *"What are the early signs that this is about to happen again?"*

Mental-Model Clarification Questions

These questions help the buyer "zoom out" and name the real category of the problem.

- *"If you zoom out a bit, how would you describe this problem?"*
- *"Does this feel more like a speed issue—or a predictability issue?"*
- *"Is this more about volume—or about signal quality?"*
- *"Do you see this as a symptom—or part of a deeper system issue?"*
- *"What do you think makes this problem so hard to solve?"*

Mini-Dialogue Example

Founder: You mentioned Engineering keeps getting blamed for delays. When priorities keep shifting upstream, what does that do to their ability to plan?

VP Product: It collapses. Everything becomes unstable.

Founder: So if we zoom out for a moment—does this feel like a speed problem, or more like an upstream stability problem?

VP Product: (*pauses*) Upstream stability. That's the real issue.

A Reframe lands when the buyer connects the dots before you say the insight out loud.

Red Flag → Green Flag

Red flag: "Your real problem isn't x—it's y."
Green flag: "When this keeps happening, what underlying pattern do you see?"

Red flag: "I think you're misdiagnosing it."
Green flag: "If we step back, what category does this issue really fall into?"

Red flag: "This is the wrong way to look at it."
Green flag: "Can I share how other teams describe this? You tell me if you see any similarities."

Reframes must feel like *their* discovery, not *your* correction.

Why These Questions Work

Reframe questions work because they create cognitive clarity at the exact moment buyers feel overwhelmed by variables, opinions, and internal politics. They reduce complexity, organize the chaos, and reveal the deeper truth hiding underneath the symptoms.

A strong Reframe lowers defensiveness and raises insight—which prepares buyers for Stage 5 (Align).

Stage 5 – Align

Questions That Build Shared Interpretation, Cross-Team Agreement & Internal Coherence

Align questions help buyers transform a *personal insight* into an *organizational insight*.

They prevent deals from dying in rooms you are not in.

Cross-Team (Shared) Interpretation Questions

These questions uncover how different groups see the same issue.

- "How would Engineering describe this problem in their own words?"
- "How does Operations see what's going on here?"
- "If Finance talked about this, what would they say the issue is?"
- "Do you think leadership sees this the same way your team does?"
- "Where do different teams see this differently?"

Alignment Gap Questions

These reveal where the internal story is inconsistent or fragmented.

- "Who already sees this as a priority—and who doesn't yet?"
- "Which team do you think is least aligned with this view?"
- "Where do you expect pushback to come from?"
- "Where could misalignment slow this down or stall it completely?"
- "Who would need more clarity before they're comfortable moving forward?"

Shared-Framing Questions

These questions help unify everyone around one coherent root cause.

- "What's a version of this problem that all teams could agree on?"
- "What's the core truth everyone seems to acknowledge, even if they phrase it differently?"
- "If you strip away team-specific language, what's really going on here?"
- "What way of talking about this would reduce friction between teams?"
- "What perspective would help everyone get on the same page?"

Mini-Dialogue Example

Founder: Engineering says capacity. Ops says process. Leadership says accountability. If we strip away roles and labels—what's the one root cause they're all pointing to?

VP Product: *(pauses)* Instability. Everything comes back to unpredictability.

Founder: If unpredictability is the shared truth, do you think talking about it that way would make it easier for everyone to align?

VP Product: Yes . . . that's the only version that actually fits all perspectives.

Alignment happens when the story becomes shared—not when one person agrees.

Red Flag → Green Flag

Red flag: "Everyone needs to get on board with this approach."

Green flag: *"How does each team see this today—and where do their views start to differ?"*

Red flag: "Let's just explain it to the leadership team."

Green flag: *"Would it be useful to look at how teams usually handle this kind of issue?"*

Red flag: "You should tell them it's a predictability issue."

Green flag: *"What's a way to describe this that teams can hear without getting defensive?"*

Alignment isn't telling people what to think—it's helping them arrive at the same understanding.

Why These Questions Work

Align questions work because buyers rarely make decisions alone. The bigger the company, the more internal narratives collide.

Engineering blames process, Ops blames workload, Leadership blames coordination.

These questions expose those fractures and gently guide the team toward **one coherent root-cause story**, so the buyer stops being a lone believer and becomes a collective one.

Alignment is the moment when insight becomes *shared reality*—opening the door to Stage 6 (Prioritize).

Stage 6 – Prioritize

Questions That Clarify Timing, Reveal Consequences & Create Natural Urgency

Prioritize questions help buyers understand the *real* timeline they are operating under.

You are not creating pressure—you are revealing it.

These questions illuminate the cost of waiting, the shrinking opportunity window, and the leadership rhythms that shape urgency.

Consequence-of-Delay Questions

These bring the hidden cost of "later" into the open—calmly and mathematically.

- "What happens if nothing changes this quarter?"
- "Who feels the impact first?"
- "What becomes harder or more expensive if this waits?"
- "Which commitments are at risk if this slips?"
- "What continues to compound if things stay as they are?"

Opportunity-Window Questions

These highlight what becomes *possible sooner* if action is taken now.

- *"If this were resolved this quarter, what would that unlock?"*
- *"Which risks start to fade once this is stabilized?"*
- *"What advantage would your team gain by moving on this now?"*
- *"What becomes easier later if this is handled first?"*
- *"What do you lose by waiting?"*

Leadership-Timing Questions

These reveal the *true internal clock* driving decisions.

- *"When is this next reviewed at the leadership level?"*
- *"Which planning or budget cycles does this run into?"*
- *"What timing matters most to the exec team right now?"*
- *"What changes if this pushes into next quarter?"*
- *"What questions will leadership ask if this isn't addressed before the next review?"*

Mini-Dialogue Example

Founder: If nothing changes this quarter, what happens to throughput consistency?

Ops Director: It stays unstable.

Founder: And who ends up carrying that instability?

Ops Director: My team. And eventually our customers.

Founder: And once customers start feeling it?

Ops Director: (*sighs*) Churn. We're already seeing early signs.

Founder: So the real decision isn't "now or later." It's "address it—or accept churn risk."

When timing connects directly to consequence, urgency appears naturally.

Red Flag → Green Flag

Red flag: "We should really move fast on this."
Green flag: "What becomes more difficult if this waits another quarter?"

Red flag: "When can you sign?"
Green flag: "When does leadership plan to revisit this topic?"

Red flag: "This is urgent."
Green flag: "What's the risk of letting this continue until Q4?"

True urgency arises from *their world*, not your pressure.

Why These Questions Work

Prioritize questions work because most buyers misjudge time. They underestimate how quickly friction compounds and how strongly leadership cycles shape when decisions can actually move.

These questions bring timing into focus without pressure. They surface consequences calmly and objectively, helping buyers see that "later" is not neutral—it carries real cost.

Prioritize is the moment when shared understanding meets reality. It turns alignment into momentum and prepares the ground for Stage 7 (Mobilize).

Stage 7 – Mobilize

Questions That Equip Champions, Navigate Politics & Win the Internal Sale

Mobilize questions help your buyer *sell the idea internally*. This is where deals are won or lost—not in your meeting, but in rooms you are not in.

These questions surface stakeholders, anticipate pushback, map internal dynamics, and help your champion carry the Reframe forward with confidence.

Mobilize is not about pressure.
It is about **equipping, protecting, and empowering** your champion.

Stakeholder Mapping Questions

These reveal who must be aligned—and who can derail momentum.

- "Who needs to feel comfortable before this moves forward?"
- "Who feels the impact of this problem most directly?"
- "Which teams are likely to have strong opinions about this?"
- *"Who usually asks the hardest questions internally?"*
- *"Who will care most about the cost of waiting?"*

Pushback Forecasting Questions

These help the buyer anticipate objections *before* they happen.

- *"Where do you expect Engineering to push back?"*
- *"What do you think Finance will question first?"*
- *"What will leadership likely scrutinize most?"*
- *"What concerns usually slow decisions like this down?"*
- *"What do you expect the strongest objection to be?"*

Internal Dynamics & Political Landscape Questions

These uncover the unspoken rules inside the organization.

- *"How do decisions like this usually get made here?"*
- *"Whose opinion carries the most weight in this situation?"*
- *"What stories or assumptions already exist about this problem?"*
- *"What other priorities could this compete with?"*
- *"What's the internal risk of leaving things as they are?"*

Champion-Confidence Questions

These ensure your buyer feels ready to advocate internally.

- *"What would help you feel fully prepared for that conversation?"*
- *"Which part of this story feels easiest to explain?"*
- *"Which part feels hardest to explain internally?"*
- *"What questions do you want to be ready for?"*
- *"Would a one-page summary help anchor the discussion?"*

Mini-Dialogue Example

Founder: Who will you need to bring this to internally?

VP Product: Engineering—and definitely our CTO.

Founder: Where do you expect Engineering to push back?

VP Product: Capacity. They'll say they don't have time.

Founder: And what will the CTO care about most?

VP Product: Strategic risk. Predictability is becoming a board-level issue.

Founder: Given that, what would help you address both perspectives clearly?

VP Product: A short, clear summary we can walk through together.

Founder: That makes sense. Something you can use to guide the conversation—not convince anyone.

This is Mobilize done correctly: not persuasion—preparation.

Red Flag → Green Flag

Red flag: "Just forward them the deck."
Green flag: *"What would help you walk them through this conversation?"*

Red flag: "You can explain the issue—it's obvious."

Green flag: *"Which part of this feels hardest to explain internally?"*

Red flag: "They should understand this by now."

Green flag: *"What do you expect leadership to question most?"*

Champions win when they feel supported, equipped, and protected.

Why These Questions Work

Mobilize questions work because decisions rarely move forward on agreement alone. They move forward when someone inside the organization is willing—and able—to carry them through internal scrutiny.

By this stage, the buyer already sees the problem clearly and agrees that something must change. What's uncertain is whether the decision can survive competing priorities, political dynamics, and leadership pressure once it leaves the room.

Mobilize questions surface those realities early. They help the buyer anticipate resistance, prepare for tough questions, and translate insight into a story that can travel across the organization.

Mobilization is the moment when clarity becomes action—opening the door to commitment.

FROM FRAMEWORK TO DAILY FOUNDER PRACTICE

Putting Buyer Sense into Practice

Below is a practical bridge between the framework and the founder's daily reality.

Most founders read sales books and think:
"Great ideas . . . but how do I actually use this tomorrow?"

Buyer Sense is different.
It's not a script.
It's not a set of tactics.
It's not a sequence of clever lines.

It's a **thinking system** designed to work in the real, messy, political, over-loaded world of modern B2B buying.

This final section gives you the four practical anchors you should keep close as you begin applying Buyer Sense Conversations in real calls.

1. The Three Rules of Modern Founder-Led Sales

These three rules preserve everything you learned across the seven stages:

Rule 1 – Safety Before Strategy

If the buyer does not feel safe, no insight will land.
Orient never ends.
You are always responsible for the emotional tone of the call.

Rule 2 – Patterns Over Individual Problems

Buyers describe symptoms.
Founders uncover systems.
Decode → Disturb → Reframe works only when you're listening
for *patterns*, not isolated incidents.

Rule 3 – Meaning Before Motion

Buyers don't move when they understand the pitch.
They move when they understand *themselves*.
Insight beats persuasion every time.

Keep these three rules visible during every call.

2. The Buyer's Real Journey (Internal, Not External)

Founders think the buyer's journey looks like:
Awareness → Consideration → Decision

Inside the company, the journey is actually:
Interpret → Align → Defend

- **Interpret:** Does this framing make sense?
- **Align:** Do others see it the same way?
- **Defend:** Can I win the internal debate?

Your seven stages map perfectly:

Internal Buyer Journey	Buyer Sense Stage
Interpret	Decode → Disturb → Reframe
Align	Align
Defend	Prioritize → Mobilize

Your job is not to "sell faster."
Your job is to **shorten the internal journey.**

3. A Weekly Founder Practice (5 Days, 15 Minutes)

This is a ritual founders use to turn Buyer Sense into muscle memory.

Monday – Orient Review

Write your Orient script for the week's top calls.
Outcome: calm, structured openings.

Tuesday – Decode Mapping

Pick one deal.
Map its upstream → downstream chain.
Outcome: deeper diagnosis.

Wednesday – Disturb Insights

List three consequences of the buyer's status quo.
Outcome: clarity, not pressure.

Thursday – Reframe Sharpening

Write one Signature Reframe for an ICP pattern.
Outcome: insight ready.

Friday – Mobilization Planning

For your top champion, map: stakeholders → objections → politics.
Outcome: deals progress instead of stall.

This is how founders integrate Buyer Sense into every conversation without overwhelm.

4. The One-Sentence Filters for Every Stage

These are "mental guardrails" you can recall instantly before each part of a call.

Stage 1 – Orient

"Make them feel safe, not sold."

Stage 2 – Decode

"Understand the system behind the symptom."

Stage 3 – Disturb

"Reveal consequence without pressure."

Stage 4 – Reframe

"Offer a mental model that makes everything click."

Stage 5 – Align

"Unify the stories across teams."

Stage 6 – Prioritize

"Show the real timeline they're already on."

Stage 7 – Mobilize

"Equip the champion to win the internal debate."

These filters act as a "quick start" mental model for every call you join.

PRACTICE RHYTHMS & HABITS

*Daily, Weekly and Monthly
Routines to Build Mastery*

How to Practice Buyer Sense Conversations

Buyer Sense Conversations is not a script—it is a skill. And like any high-leverage skill (diagnosis, analysis, sensemaking), it sharpens through **rhythm**, not effort.

Many founders struggle not because they lack ability, but because they lack a **practice system**.

This section gives you a simple, realistic routine for embedding Buyer Sense into your daily work.
No overwhelm.
No over-preparation.
Just consistent calibration.

Daily Practice (10 minutes)

Goal: Keep the seven stages "alive" in your mind before every call.

1. **Preview the next call.**

   - Which stage are you likely to spend most time in?
   - What outcome needs to emerge?

2. **Choose two to three core questions.**

These are not scripts—they are *anchors* for clarity and direction.

3. **Name the transition you're waiting for.**

   - "Buyer relaxes" → move from Orient → Decode
   - "Root cause is understood" → move from Decode → Disturb
   - "Realization moment" → move from Disturb → Reframe

4. **Set your tone.**
   Calm. Neutral. Investigative.
   You lead the room by stabilizing it.

Why this matters:
Micro-reps create conversational muscle memory.
You enter calls with intention instead of improvisation.

Weekly Practice – The Pipeline Review (Founder Style)

Goal: Sense where each deal *really* is—not where CRM stages say it is.

Run a 30-minute weekly ritual:

1. **List all active opportunities**
2. For each deal, ask:

   - "Which stage did the last call end in?"
   - "Did we complete that stage's transition signals?"
   - "What is the *next* stage this buyer actually needs?"

3. Rewrite your follow-up emails so they:

   - Match the correct stage
   - Pull the buyer forward instead of pushing them ahead

Example:
If the buyer is misaligned internally, you are not in Prioritize.
You are stuck in **Align**, and your next move must reflect that.

Why this matters:
Many stalled deals are simply in the wrong stage.
Weekly stage correction keeps your pipeline honest.

Monthly Practice – Reflection & Skill Reps

Goal: Sharpen pattern recognition across multiple conversations.

Once per month, do a short retrospective:

1. Analyze 5 recent calls

Ask yourself:

- Where did buyers open up?
- Where did the energy drop?
- Which stage transitions were smooth?
- Where did you push too early?

2. Document 3–5 new patterns

These could be:

- Upstream triggers
- Hidden friction points
- Leadership concerns
- Cross-team contradictions
- Timing windows buyers missed

Patterns become your strategic advantage.

3. Update your "signature" Reframes

Founder mastery comes from refining the 3–5 Reframes buyers
respond to over and over.
These evolve monthly.

4. Improve one stage intentionally

Rotate monthly:

- January → Decode mastery
- February → Disturb clarity
- March → Mobilize narrative building

This keeps you sharp without overwhelming you.

Why this matters:
Monthly reflection builds compound clarity.
Over time, your conversations become faster, cleaner, and deeper—without effort.

Quarterly Practice – The Sensemaking Upgrade

Goal: Elevate your whole system, not just your next call.

Every quarter:

1. **Review all closed-won deals**

   - Which stage unlocked them?
   - What convinced internal decision-makers?
   - Which questions worked best?

2. **Review all closed-lost deals**

   - At which stage did the breakdown occur?
   - Which signals were missing?
   - What would you do differently now?

3. **Update your internal Buyer Sense playbook**

   - New patterns
   - New examples
   - New political dynamics
   - Updated Reframes and alignment maps

4. **Train your team**
   Teach your team one stage per quarter.
   Start with Decode → Disturb → Reframe → Mobilize.

Why this matters:
Quarterly upgrades make Buyer Sense a company capability—
not a founder dependency.

Your New Rhythm as a Sensemaker

Daily = mindset
Weekly = pipeline truth
Monthly = skill sharpening
Quarterly = system evolution

Mastery doesn't come from pressure.
It comes from deliberate, calm, repeated sensemaking.

This rhythm turns Buyer Sense Conversations
from a framework you understand
into a foundation you *embody*.

THE FOUNDER PLAYBOOK

The Seven Stages on One Page

This is a short mental model founders can use before every call to unlock clarity, timing, and internal momentum.[32]

This is the operational map of Buyer Sense.
Use it before a call, during a call, or as a quick reset when you feel the conversation drifting.

Asset 4: The Buyer Sense Playbook

This asset is where Buyer Sense turns into **execution**.

Here you'll find the practical tools and templates that support real conversations—before calls, after calls, and during internal buyer discussions. These are not theoretical frameworks. They are working materials designed to help you structure thinking, clarify next steps, and equip buyer champions.

This asset includes:

- The Buyer Sense Playbook (seven stages on one page)
- Practical tools such as maps, ladders, and checklists
- Fill-in-the-blank templates for founders and champions

Use this asset when:

---

32. Gartner, "Sensemaking Sellers," 2020 – sensemaking improves buyer momentum by ~2x.

- Preparing for an important call
- Reviewing a stalled deal
- Helping a buyer align stakeholders internally
- Translating insight into internal action

These tools are meant to be **printed, reused, and adapted**. Use what you need, when you need it—without trying to use everything at once.

1. Orient – Create Safety & Structure

Goal: Make the buyer feel safe, understood, and in control.
Your mindset: *"No pressure. Pure clarity."*

What to do:

- Set a clear focus for the conversation
- Explain why you're meeting and how you'll use the time
- Show that you've prepared and respect their context
- Remove any sense of pressure or pitch
- Ask what would make the conversation valuable today

Buyer should feel:
"Good—this will be useful and safe."

2. Decode – Reveal How Their World Actually Works

Goal: Understand the system, not the symptom.
Your mindset: *"Explore the workflow, not the pain."*

What to do:

- Walk through real processes as they happen day to day
- Trace what sets issues in motion and how they spread
- Uncover friction, instability, and hidden effort
- Follow problems as they move across teams and over time

Buyer should think:
"They really understand how our world works."

3. Disturb – Reveal Consequences Calmly

Goal: Make the real cost of the status quo visible.
Your mindset: *"Clarity, not pressure."*

What to do:

- Explore what happens when the problem continues
- Bring hidden risks and trade-offs into view
- Show how issues repeat and spread over time
- Name what quietly becomes harder if nothing changes

Buyer should say:
"We can't keep doing it this way."

4. Reframe – Shift Their Mental Model

Goal: Give the buyer a clearer, more truthful interpretation.
Your mindset: *"Insight, not cleverness."*

What to do:

- Start from how the problem shows up day to day
- Connect the dots between related issues
- Show how the same pattern appears across teams or situations
- Offer a simpler way to understand what's really going on

Buyer should say:
"That actually explains everything."

5. Align – Build Shared Understanding Across Stakeholders

Goal: Turn individual understanding into organizational alignment.
Your mindset: *"Unify the narrative."*

What to do:

- Surface how different teams see the same problem.

- Bring conflicting views into the open without judgment.
- Help teams agree on what actually matters and why.
- Connect the new understanding to a direction everyone can support.

Buyer should think:
"We all see this the same way."

6. Prioritize – Clarify Timing & Consequences of Waiting

Goal: Reveal the true timeline the buyer is actually on.
Your mindset: *"Reveal the clock, don't create one."*

What to do:

- Explore what changes if the decision is delayed.
- Surface what becomes possible if action happens sooner.
- Connect timing to planning, budget, and leadership rhythms.
- Help the buyer see that waiting has consequences.

Buyer should say:
"We can't wait—the timing matters."

7. Mobilize – Equip Your Champion to Win Internally

Goal: Make the buyer strong enough to carry the story without you.
Your mindset: *"Don't sell harder—empower smarter."*

What to do:

- Identify who needs to be involved and who might slow things down.
- Anticipate questions, concerns, and resistance.
- Help shape a clear, repeatable story the buyer can use internally.
- Prepare simple materials that support the conversation.
- Make the buyer feel prepared for internal discussion and scrutiny.

Buyer should feel:
"I can win the internal case."

The Meta Flow of Seven Stages

Orient → Decode → Disturb → Reframe → Align → Prioritize → Mobilize

Each stage sets up the next.
If one is weak, all downstream stages collapse.

Use this one-page playbook as your quick-start before every call.

BUYER SENSE FAILURE MODES

The 5 Patterns That Break Conversations (and How to Prevent Them)

Figure 10 below illustrates the most common patterns that disrupt Buyer Sense Conversations during real sales interactions. Each failure mode represents a breakdown in sensemaking—where the founder moves ahead of the buyer, applies pressure, or loses awareness of internal dynamics. Conversations stall not because the solution is wrong, but because the flow is broken. Buyer Sense succeeds when the founder recognizes these patterns early and restores the conversation to the appropriate stage.

Even the strongest founders—the strategic, prepared, thoughtful ones—fall into predictable traps during real conversations.

Buyer Sense Conversations only work when the **flow is protected**.

Here we'll discuss the **5 failure modes** that break the flow, stall deals, and destroy buyer trust.

For each one, you'll see:

- What the founder does
- What the buyer experiences
- How the deal derails
- How to fix it instantly (Sensemaking-style)

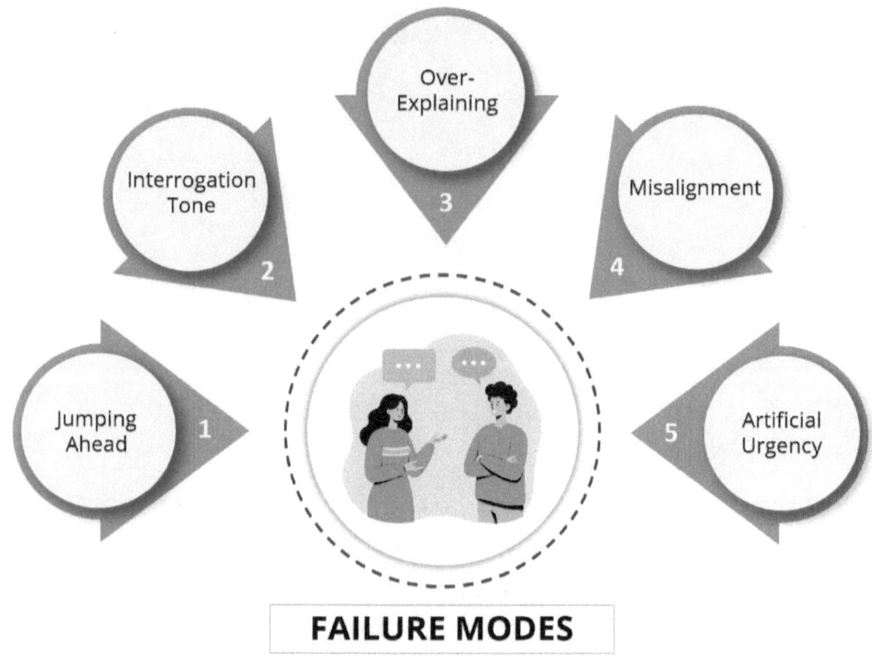

Figure 10: Failure Modes

Failure Mode 1 – Jumping Ahead of the Buyer

Skipping stages, collapsing stages, or trying to compress them into one.

What founders do:

- Reframe too early
- Disturb before Decode is complete
- Prioritize before alignment
- Mobilize a buyer who isn't ready

What the buyer experiences:

- Pressure
- Confusion
- "This person is pushing me somewhere I'm not yet at."

How the deal breaks: The buyer retreats into guarded answers, politeness, or delays.

Fix (Sensmaking Style): Ask yourself before advancing:

"Has the buyer given me the signal that this stage is complete?" If not, stay exactly where you are.

Failure Mode 2 – Turning Questions into Interrogation

The founder sounds like a salesperson gathering ammunition.

What founders do:

- Machine-gun questions
- Rapid-fire sequencing
- Overuse "why"
- Jumping from topic to topic without flow

What the buyer experiences:

- Being tested
- Being analyzed
- Feeling unsafe

How the deal breaks: Buyers offer surface-level answers → no insight → no Reframe → no alignment.

Fix (Sensmaking Style): Slow the tempo. Replace "why" with:
"Walk me through what happened."
"What usually triggers that?"

The tone becomes exploration instead of interrogation.

Failure Mode 3 – Over-Explaining or Over-Selling

Talking too much, too early, or in the wrong moments.

What founders do:

- Jump into monologues

- Enter "teaching mode" too soon
- Defend their interpretation
- Talk over buyer signals

What the buyer experiences:

- Loss of clarity
- Loss of agency
- Feeling like a pitch is coming

How the deal breaks: The buyer stops thinking and starts evaluating—which kills discovery momentum.

Fix (Sensmaking Style): Use the **Conversation Ratio Rule**: Buyer talks 70 percent. Founder talks 30 percent. If you hear yourself speaking for more than **20 seconds,** stop and return to a question.

Failure Mode 4 – Mismanaging Cross-Functional Perspectives

Aligning with one person, ignoring the system.

What founders do:

- Treat the buyer's opinion as the organization's truth
- Assume one champion = full alignment
- Ignore Engineering, Finance, Ops, or Leadership perspectives
- Skip stakeholder mapping

What the buyer experiences:

- Being left to fight internal battles alone
- Political risk
- Pressure to "sell internally"

How the deal breaks: The deal collapses in internal meetings you never attend.

Fix (Sensmaking Style): Ask early:

"Who else sees this problem differently?"

"What would Finance/Ops/Engineering push back on?"

Never assume one voice = the system.

Failure Mode 5 – Trying to Create Urgency Instead of Revealing It

Artificial pressure destroys trust.

What founders do:

- Push timelines
- Manufacture urgency
- Threaten opportunity loss
- Try to "close" instead of clarify

What the buyer experiences:

- Manipulation
- Resistance
- Emotional withdrawal

How the deal breaks: The buyer delays out of self-protection.

Fix (Sensmaking Style): Reveal the **real** timeline hiding in their system:
"What happens if nothing changes this quarter?"
"When is your next leadership review on this topic?"

Urgency emerges from **their world**, not yours.

The Meta-Failure Behind All Failure Modes: Losing the Thread

There is one failure mode beneath all others:

The founder stops sensemaking and starts selling.

The moment the mindset shifts from:

"I want to understand your world . . ."

to

"I want you to choose my product . . ."

The entire Buyer Sense flow collapses.

BUYER SENSE TOOLS (QUICK REFERENCE)

This is an index of every tool inside the seven stages. Nothing new—just your grab-and-go toolbox.

These are the tools introduced throughout the book, organized in one place so founders can find them fast when preparing for real calls.

How to Use This Section

This is your **quick-access guide to tools** for real conversations.

Stage 1 – Orient Tools

- The Orient Script (1-minute opener)
- Buyer Safety Signals Checklist
- Preparation Checklist (before the call)

Stage 2 – Decode Tools

- The Workflow Mapping Template
- Upstream—Downstream Chain
- Hidden Friction Finder
- Decode Question Sequence Builder

Stage 3 – Disturb Tools

- The Consequence Chain
- Hidden Risk Map (Operational/Strategic/Relationship
- Gentle Disturb Questions
- Tone Guardrails Checklist

Stage 4 – Reframe Tools

- Signature Reframe Builder
- Sector Reframe Examples
- Pattern Framework (Resource → Flow, Speed → Predictability, etc.)

Stage 5 – Align Tools

- Alignment Map (Personal → Functional → Strategic)
- Stakeholder Interpretation Grid
- Co-Building Criteria Script

Stage 6 – Prioritize Tools

- Prioritization Map (Consequence/Opportunity/Timing)
- The Consequence Ladder
- Non-Pressure Timeline Questions

Stage 7 – Mobilize Tools

- Internal Champion Narrative (1-page template)
- Stakeholder Map
- Political Risk Radar
- Champion Confidence Ladder

BUYER SENSE TEMPLATES

Practical, fill-in-the-blank templates you can use before, during, or after calls.
Designed for founders, teams, and champions.

Template 1: Orient Script (Fill in the Blanks)

Purpose: Create safety, structure, and control.

Thanks for making the time today. I prepared by reviewing

______________________ _______________________

so we can stay focused on what matters most.

Here's what I suggest for the next _______ minutes:

1) ______________________________________

2) ______________________________________

3) ______________________________________

Before we dive in, what would make this conversation valuable for you today?

Signal to proceed: Buyer relaxes, agrees to the structure, adds what matters.

Template 2: Decode – Workflow Mapping Sheet

Purpose: Understand how work actually flows.

What triggers the workflow? __________________________

Step-by-step flow:

1) ____

2) ____

3) ____

Upstream triggers: _______________________________

Downstream impacts: ______________________________

Hidden friction points: ___________________________

Who absorbs the friction? _________________________

What becomes unpredictable? ______________________

Template 3: Disturb – Consequence Chain Worksheet

Purpose: Reveal the real cost of the status quo calmly.

When this issue occurs, what breaks first? ______________

Then what breaks next? ______________________________

Who absorbs the impact? _____________________________

What becomes harder or more expensive? ______________

What becomes impossible if this continues for another quarter?

____

Template 4: Reframe – Signature Reframe Builder

Purpose: Shift the buyer's mental model.

Their symptom (in their words): ______________________

Hidden root cause: _________________________________

Pattern across similar companies: ____________________

Simple mental model: ______________________________

Your signature Reframe sentence:

"You don't have a ______________ issue—you have a ______________ issue."

Template 5: Align – Stakeholder Alignment Map

Purpose: Create shared understanding across the organization.

Who experiences the impact? ______________________________

How each team interprets the problem:

- Product: ______________________________

- Engineering: ______________________________

- Operations: ______________________________

- Finance: ______________________________

- Leadership: ______________________________

Shared truth all teams can agree on: ______________________

Co-built criteria for moving forward: ______________________

Template 6: Prioritize – Timing & Consequence Worksheet

Purpose: Reveal the real timeline and cost of waiting.

If nothing changes this quarter, what happens? ______________

Who absorbs the impact first? ______________________

What becomes harder or more expensive later? ______________

Opportunity window:

"What becomes possible if we solve this now?" _______________

Leadership timing anchors:

- Next review: _________________________________ ________

- Budget cycle: _________________________________ ________

- Delivery window: _______________________________ ________

Template 7: Mobilize – Internal Champion 1-Pager

Purpose: Help your champion win the internal debate.

1. Problem summary (the Reframe):

____

2. Evidence (workflow + patterns):

____

3. Consequences of waiting:

____

4. Opportunity if solved now:

____

5. Solution type (category alignment):

____

6. Fit with strategic priorities:

____

7. Next internal step:

____

FINAL REFLECTION QUESTIONS

This is a guided self-assessment to strengthen your Buyer Sense identity.

Buyer Sense Conversations is not just a method. It is a skill, a mindset, and ultimately an identity.

These reflection questions help you integrate the seven stages into your daily behavior, so the flow becomes natural—not performative.

Take time with them.
They work best when answered honestly and without judgment.

1. Your Founder Mindset

- What part of conversations makes you feel most confident today—and why?
- What part still triggers tension or pressure inside you?
- When do you shift from "sensemaking" to "selling"?
- What belief about sales do you now want to retire?
- What belief about buyers do you want to replace it with?

2. Your Conversation Patterns

- Which stage of the seven-stage flow do you naturally excel at?
- Which stage do you tend to rush or skip—and what happens when you do?
- When have you recently jumped ahead of the buyer?

- What signals do you now see that tell you: "Stay here longer"?

3. Your Buyer Impact

- What is one moment recently where a buyer said something revealing and you missed it?
- What is one moment where your calmness created trust?
- Which of your questions consistently unlocks truth for buyers?
- Which question do you want to stop using because it creates pressure?

4. Your System Awareness

- What patterns do you now see more clearly in buyer workflows?
- Where do buyers consistently misdiagnose their own problems?
- What friction or consequence do they underestimate most often?
- How does their system create the timing pressure they don't yet see?

5. Your Alignment Skill

- When did you mistake personal alignment for organizational alignment?
- Who are the silent influencers you tend to overlook?
- How could you unify conflicting narratives faster next time?
- What would help buyers align with each other without you in the room?

6. Your Timing Intelligence

- What question helped you reveal the real timeline most effectively?
- Where did you avoid talking about timing—and why?

- Looking at your current pipeline:
- Who is actually urgent?
- Who only *feels* urgent?
- Who is hiding behind "later"?

7. Your Champion Support

- Who in your current deals is becoming your strongest champion—and why?
- What support do they need that you haven't given yet?
- What version of a one-page internal narrative could change their momentum?
- What political risk are they facing that you must help them navigate?

8. Your Growth Path

- Which stage of Buyer Sense will you practice deliberately next week?
- What skill—question, tone, sequence—will you make your "micro-focus"?
- What will you look for in real calls to track your progress?
- What does "Buyer Sense Mastery" look like for you in 90 days?

9. Your New Identity

- If you lived as a **Buyer Sensemaker** from tomorrow onward:

  - How would you enter the call?
  - How would you listen?
  - How would you guide?
  - How would you reveal truth without pressure?
  - How would you help buyers win internally?

Write 3 sentences that describe your new sales identity:

These sentences become your compass.

    1.

    2.

    3.

YOUR NEW IDENTITY: BUYER SENSEMAKER

For years, founders have been told that sales is a performance. They were taught to persuade, to push, to master closing techniques, and to create urgency where none exists. The underlying message was always the same: selling is something you do to a buyer. But the modern B2B world no longer rewards that approach. Buyers are overloaded, politically entangled, and under immense pressure to make defensible decisions in environments where everything feels uncertain. They do not want to be convinced. They want to be understood. They want someone who can make sense of their world.

Throughout this book, you were shown a different path—one rooted in truth, clarity, and calm authority. It is a path where founders succeed not by selling harder, but by thinking more clearly. It is a path where sales becomes an act of leadership, not performance. When you follow this path, you become something far more powerful than a traditional salesperson. You become a Sensemaker.

A Buyer Sensemaker is not a performer or a persuader. A Sensemaker is someone who can sit inside a buyer's messy reality, absorb the complexity, and bring order to it. You translate chaos into coherence, symptoms into systems, noise into insight, and confusion into confidence. Most importantly, you help buyers make decisions they can defend—even when you are not in the room. That ability is the highest form of commercial influence, and it is the foundation of all modern, trust-based selling.

Across these chapters, you have learned a framework that reshapes how founders talk to buyers: Orient, Decode, Disturb, Reframe, Align, Prioritize, Mobilize. This is no longer simply a meeting structure. It is a mental model—a new way of seeing buyer behavior, guiding decisions, and shaping internal dynamics.

Each stage has rewired how you think. Orient showed you how to create psychological safety so buyers can think freely. Decode taught you to uncover systems instead of chasing symptoms. Disturb revealed how to surface consequences without pressure. Reframe gave you a way to provide clarity that feels true and relieving. Align helped you unify fragmented internal narratives. Prioritize showed you how to reveal timing without manipulation. Mobilize taught you how to equip champions for the internal conversations that ultimately determine the outcome of the deal. These are not tactics. They are leadership behaviors. And they are the reason Buyer Sense Conversations transforms founders into trusted commercial partners.

As you move forward, three transformations matter most. The first is the shift from seller to sensemaker. You no longer chase answers; you create clarity. The second is the shift from storyteller to truth-revealer. You no longer try to convince; you help buyers see their world more accurately. The third is the shift from vendor to strategic advisor. You no longer pitch; you guide decisions. These transformations cannot be unlearned. Once you see conversations this way, you can never return to the old model.

You are no longer the founder who tries to sell. You are the founder who sees systems buyers cannot see, names risks they underestimate, Reframes problems they misinterpret, builds alignment they cannot build alone, reveals timing they do not realize they are on, and equips champions to win internal battles. You bring clarity to complexity, calm to tension, direction to confusion, and confidence to hesitant buyers. You are a Buyer Sensemaker. Carry this identity with you into every call, every meeting, every leadership review, every negotiation. Founders who master sensemaking don't just win deals—they become the kind of leaders buyers trust, teams follow, and companies grow around.

There is only one step left. Do not let Buyer Sense remain theory. Turn it into a habit. Make it your default. Practice it until it becomes instinct. The next time you step into a customer conversation, pause for a moment and ask yourself one simple question: *"Am I here to sell—or am I here to make sense?"* Choose sense. Every time. It will change your trajectory more than any tactic ever could.

This is your new identity. Your new edge. Your new advantage as a founder. You are now—and from this point forward—a Buyer Sensemaker.

ABOUT THE AUTHOR

Petra Wagner is an international sales strategist, a founder coach, and the creator of the SalesBooster™ and Buyer Sense Conversations frameworks—modern systems designed to help early-stage founders close meaningful deals with clarity, confidence, and integrity.

Her career began far from the meeting rooms she now coaches founders to master.

As a competitive Latin American and ballroom dancer, Petra won the **Junior Blackpool Championship**, one of the world's most prestigious dance titles. As a coach, she learned discipline, presence, timing, and human behavior—skills that later became core to her philosophy of modern, human-first sales.

After completing degrees in **Sociology and Pedagogy**, Petra joined **IBM**, where she built a reputation for strategic thinking, partner orchestration, and enterprise relationship leadership. She held roles across **key account management**, **regional leadership**, and **IBM Global Financing**, earning the **Best Sales Award at IBM**.

She later joined **Microsoft** as a Sales Manager and Regional Sales Leader, driving growth across enterprise, SMB, and corporate segments. Her work in the Microsoft partner ecosystem, co-selling motions, and regional go-to-market strategy gave her deep expertise in **partner orchestration**, **digital transformation**, and **complex deal navigation**.

After two decades on the seller side, Petra made a rare transition—becoming an **enterprise buyer and transformation leader** inside a large traditional company. There, she experienced firsthand the emotional, political, and cognitive overload buyers face every day. That experience changed everything. She realized founders weren't struggling because their products lacked value—they were struggling because they didn't know how to guide buyers toward clarity.

This realization became the foundation of her own practice. Petra combined her enterprise experience, partner ecosystem expertise, academic training, startup advisory work, and buyer-side insight to create **SalesBooster™** and **Buyer Sense Conversations™**, two practical, human-first frameworks now trusted by tech founders across Europe and beyond.

Her mission is simple:

To help founders sell in a way that feels human, structured, and honest—so sales becomes less random and far more repeatable.

Startups work with Petra because she brings a rare 360° perspective: **seller → leader → partner strategist → enterprise buyer → founder coach.**

She knows exactly what happens on both sides of the table and teaches founders how to navigate the messy, political, emotionally complex reality of modern B2B buying with clarity and confidence.

Petra lives in **Slovenia** with her partner and three children. Outside of coaching, she is an avid skier, kitesurfer, runner, and gym enthusiast—always in motion, always learning, always pushing into new frontiers, just like the founders she supports.

SOURCES & REFERENCES

This book blends Petra Wagner's two decades of enterprise leadership, coaching experience, and founder advisory work with leading research on commercial decision-making, buying psychology, sensemaking, and modern B2B behavior.

This research supports the psychology, buyer behavior, and commercial decision-making patterns described in Buyer Sense Conversations™. All proprietary methodologies (including the Seven Stages, Internal Buyer Journey™, Reframe Structures, and Champion Maps) originate from Petra Wagner.

1. Research Firms & Industry Reports

Gartner/CEB (now Gartner)

- *The B2B Buying Journey* (2019–2023) — B2B buying is nonlinear, high-stakes, and involves multiple stakeholders; 77% of buyers describe purchases as complex.
- *Buyer Enablement Research* (2016–2021) — Information overload increases no-decision outcomes; decision support matters more than persuasion.
- *Winning the Consensus Sale* (2016) — High-stakes B2B decisions require internal alignment and shared confidence.
- *Boost Buyer Confidence to Drive High-Quality Deals* (2021) — Buyer confidence is the strongest predictor of deal progression.
- *Sensemaking Sellers* (2020) — Sensemaking behaviors double buyer momentum.
- *Future of Sales* (2025) — Buyers receive less than 20% of

information directly from vendors; orchestration and emotional safety drive outcomes.

McKinsey & Company

- *The New B2B Buying Landscape* (2020) — Hybrid, multi-threaded buying processes.
- *The B2B Decision-Making Paradox* (2020) — Organizational friction slows buying more than competition.
- *The New B2B Growth Equation* (2021–2022) — 6–11 stakeholders per deal; shared understanding drives conversion.

Forrester Research

- *Emotional Drivers in B2B Buying* (2021) — Emotional confidence predicts purchase outcomes.
- *How B2B Buyers Make Decisions* (2022) — Trust, clarity, and internal risk shape decisions.
- Research on executive decision risk and internal exposure — Fear of internal blame blocks progress.

2. Foundational Books & Academic Research

- Ainslie, G. (1975). *Specious Reward*. Psychological Bulletin — Hyperbolic discounting and short-term bias.
- Bandura, A. (1997). *Self-Efficacy: The Exercise of Control.* — Confidence and perceived capability.
- Bazerman, M. H., & Moore, D. A. (2012). *Judgment in Managerial Decision Making.* — Bias and decision traps.
- Brehm, J. W. (1966). *A Theory of Psychological Reactance.* — Resistance to pressure.
- Cyert, R. M., & March, J. G. (1963). *A Behavioral Theory of the Firm.* — Organizational decision limits.
- Kahneman, D. (2011). *Thinking, Fast and Slow.* — Cognitive overload, loss aversion.
- Kahneman, D., & Tversky, A. (1979). *Prospect Theory.* Econometrica — Buyers overweight potential losses.

- Mintzberg, H. (1983). *Power In and Around Organizations.* — Internal politics.
- Mintzberg, H., Raisinghani, D., & Théorêt, A. (1976). *The Structure of "Unstructured" Decision Processes.* — Nonlinear decisions.
- Pfeffer, J. (1992). *Managing with Power.* — Influence and internal alignment.
- Rogers, E. M. (2003). *Diffusion of Innovations.* — Adoption dynamics.
- Simon, H. A. (1997). *Administrative Behavior.* — Bounded rationality.
- Sweller, J. (1988). *Cognitive Load During Problem Solving.* — Cognitive overload effects.
- Weick, K. E. (1995). *Sensemaking in Organizations.* — Meaning-making under ambiguity.

3. Articles & Journals

Harvard Business Review

- *Why Your Customers Don't Want to Innovate* (2021–2022) — Career risk inhibits change.
- *The Hidden Risk in B2B Decisions* (2022) — Internal exposure outweighs ROI.
- *The HBR Manager's Handbook* (2017) — Leadership decision skills.

MIT Sloan Management Review

- *When Coordination Fails: The Systems-Thinking Solution* (2019) — Upstream system flaws drive downstream friction.

4. Sales & Commercial Methodology

- Adamson, B., & Dixon, M. (2011). *The Challenger Sale.* — Insight-led selling.
- Adamson, B., & Schmidt, M. (2022). *The JOLT Effect.* — 40–60% of pipeline loss stems from indecision.

- Adamson, B., & Schmidt, M. (2025). *The Framemaking Sale.* — Shared frames reduce no-decision outcomes.

5. Contemporary Models & Industry Observations

- LinkedIn / Taurus RevGen — Nonlinear buying behavior.
- Gartner buyer misalignment and buyer enablement models.

6. Proprietary Frameworks & Original Intellectual Property

The following frameworks are original work by **Petra Wagner** and form the structural backbone of this book:

- SalesBooster™ Methodology
- Buyer Sense Conversations™ Framework
- Seven-Stage Buyer Sense Flow
- Internal Buyer Journey™ (Interpret → Align → Defend)
- Alignment Layers™
- Consequence Ladder™
- Mobilize Champion Map™
- Signature Reframe Structures

These frameworks are based on over **twenty years of enterprise leadership, sales, and transformation experience** at IBM, Microsoft, and in founder advisory roles.

www.ingramcontent.com/pod-product-compliance
Lightning Source LLC
Chambersburg PA
CBHW030900060726
47591CB00005B/1354